A Church for All Peoples
Missionary Issues in a World Church

Joseph Augustine DiNoia, O.P.
Avery Dulles, S.J.
Francis E. George, O.M.I.
Joan Frances Gormley, S.S.M.W.
Eugene LaVerdiere, S.S.S.
William J. McCormack
J. Francis Stafford

Edited by
Eugene LaVerdiere, S.S.S.

A Liturgical Press Book

THE LITURGICAL PRESS
Collegeville, Minnesota

Cover design by Greg Becker

Copyright © 1993 by The Order of St. Benedict, Inc., Collegeville, Minnesota. All rights reserved. No part of this book may be reproduced in any form or by any means, electronic or mechanical, including photocopying, recording, taping, or any retrieval system, without the written permission of The Liturgical Press, Collegeville, Minnesota 56321. Printed in the United States of America.

1   2   3   4   5   6   7   8   9

Library of Congress Cataloging-in-Publication Data

A Church for all peoples : missionary issues in a world church / edited by Eugene LaVerdiere.
    p.   cm.
  Papers originally presented at a symposium: The Church: salvation and mission, Oct. 1991.
  Includes index.
  ISBN 0-8146-2141-4
  1. Catholic Church—Missions—Congresses. 2. Missions—Theory--Congresses. 3. Christianity and culture—Congresses.
I. LaVerdiere, Eugene.
BV2160.C48 1993
266'.2—dc20   93-9678
                                                                         CIP

Contents

Foreword *William J. McCormack, D.D.*	5
Preface *Eugene LaVerdiere, S.S.S.*	8
I. The Church and the Kingdom *Avery Dulles, S.J.*	13
Response *Francis E. George, O.M.I.*	27
II. The Inscrutable Riches of Christ: The Catholic Church's Mission of Salvation *J. Francis Stafford, D.D.*	31
Response *Joseph Augustine DiNoia, O.P.*	51
III. The Church and Cultures *Francis E. George, O.M.I.*	55
Response *J. Francis Stafford, D.D.*	70
IV. The Church and Dialogue with Other Religions: A Plea for the Recognition of Differences *Joseph Augustine DiNoia, O.P.*	75
Response *Avery Dulles, S.J.*	89

Missionary Issues in a World Church   93
Reflective Synthesis
  Joan Frances Gormley, S.S.M.W.

Authors   100

Index   102

Foreword

On behalf of my brother bishops of the Committee on the Missions of the National Conference of Catholic Bishops, I welcome the publication of the presentations delivered at the symposium on *The Church: Salvation and Mission.* The symposium, which was held at the Center for Development in Ministry in Mundelein, Illinois, on October 11–13, 1991, brought together distinguished theologians and educators, superiors of missionary communities and their representatives, as well as diocesan directors of the Society for the Propagation of the Faith and the Holy Childhood Association, all of whom have key leadership responsibilities in the Church for the essential task of fostering a vital missionary spirit. That missionary spirit characterizes and expresses the very nature of the Church and is, and must be, the dynamic of her entire apostolate.

The symposium coincided with the fifth anniversary of the publication of the U.S. Bishops' Pastoral Statement on World Missions, *To the Ends of the Earth,* which was written to help stimulate interest in and a personal sense of responsibility for the Church's mission to others and to affirm missionaries in their efforts to proclaim the gospel and promote the reign of God.

In his encyclical, *On the Permanent Validity of the Church's Missionary Mandate, Redemptoris missio,* Pope John Paul foresees, in his words, "the dawning of a new missionary age." Paradoxically, however, the Pope speaks of "an undeniable negative tendency," which his letter is intended to address. "Missionary activity specifically directed 'to the nations,'" John Paul says, "appears to be waning. . . . Difficulties both internal and external have weakened the Church's missionary thrust towards non-Christians." The Pope calls this diminishing of missionary vitality "a sign of a crisis of faith."

The encyclical includes in these internal questions the role of the

Church in the universal salvation towards which all human beings are ordered. There is a need to integrate the two concepts of the real possibility of salvation for each member of the human family and, at the same time, the necessity of the Church for salvation.

Other areas of major concern addressed by the Holy Father include the relationship of Church and kingdom, the necessity and true purpose of dialogue, and the authentic inculturation of the gospel in today's increasingly interdependent and secular world. These are precisely the areas treated in the papers which are now being made available to a wider audience.

If the Pope can speak in the same document of his vision of "the dawning of a new missionary age" and of his perception of the waning of missionary activity on behalf of non-Christians, I believe the paradox can be resolved in light of the encyclical's section on missionary spirituality. Here we are reminded that missionary motivation, activity, and fruitfulness are all the work of the Holy Spirit. The missionary nature of the Church is dynamically rooted in the Trinitarian mission itself. In other words, it depends on us, but only up to a point. As the Lord tells us through Isaiah: "The word that goes from my mouth does not return to me empty, without carrying out my will and succeeding in what it was sent to do" (Isa 55:11).

The universal missionary spirit and activity which each of us is called by the Church to articulate and encourage has but one purpose, as Pope John Paul says: to serve human beings by revealing to them the love of God made manifest in Jesus Christ. The importance and urgency of our task is made clear by the Holy Father in these words: "For each believer, as for the entire Church, the missionary task must remain foremost, for it concerns the eternal destiny of humanity and corresponds to God's mysterious and merciful plan."

We are most fortunate to have had as presenters at the symposium distinguished authorities in each of the four major theological areas that challenge missionary activity today. I know I speak for all the participants in expressing gratitude to them for the great amount of time and effort they expended in preparing the papers for the meeting and for this publication.

I am grateful to Sr. Joan Gormley, of the Sisters of St. Mary of Washington, for accepting the formidable challenge of providing a synthesis and conclusion for the symposium. I am grateful to the staff director of the Missions Committee, N.C.C.B., Dr. David Byers, and to my own staff in New York, most especially Mary McLoughlin. I am grateful to Fr. Eugene LaVerdiere, of the Congregation of the Blessed Sacrament, who provided the inspiration and the plan for the symposium and has followed up with the publication of what I am convinced is a significant contribution to mission theology in the Church today.

Finally, I am most grateful to Sr. Janet Carroll of Maryknoll who graciously acted as a facilitator for the symposium.

Most Reverend William J. McCormack, D.D.
March 1, 1992

Preface

Until recently, hardly anyone alluded to the missionary nature of the Church. There was no need. Mission was in fact at the center of the Church, and its missionary nature could fairly well be taken for granted. Mission was seen as a normal expression of a mature Church, as it was in the forties of the first century, when the Church at Antioch first sent Barnabas and Paul to preach the gospel on Cyprus and in what is now southern Turkey. So it has been through much of the history of the Church. It never occurred to Francis Xavier, Isaac Jogues, and a host of others to question the validity or the worth of the missionary enterprise.

In modern times, it took one hundred years from the writing of the first encyclical by Benedict XIV in 1740 (*Ubi primum, On the Duties of the Bishop*) to the first encyclical on world mission by Gregory XVI in 1840 (*Probe nostes, On the Propagation of the Faith*). From Leo XIII to John XXIII, an additional five encyclicals have addressed the subject, all of them promoting the Church's missionary effort and dealing with various issues associated with it, but always assuming its validity. For example, in his encyclical *Princeps pastorum* (November 28, 1959), John XXIII dealt with the development of a native clergy and the participation of the laity in the work of the Church, but found no need to defend the legitimacy of the Church's mission.

Today, as in many other areas of Church life, the situation has changed, and Pope John Paul II found it necessary to issue an encyclical *On the Permanent Validity of the Church's Missionary Mandate, Redemptoris missio* (December 7, 1990). "Missionary evangelization," says the Pope, is "the primary service which the Church can render to every individual and to all humanity in the modern world" (2). This extraordinary statement situates missionary commitment and activity at the very center of church life. With Vatican II's Decree on the

Church's Missionary Activity (*Ad gentes* 2), the Pope describes the Church as missionary by its very nature: "The missionary thrust therefore belongs to the very nature of the Christian life" (1) and is crucial for renewing the Church, revitalizing faith, and strengthening Christian identity (2).

So much insistence means that the missionary nature of the Church can no longer be taken for granted. More than that, most observers would agree that there are strong forces at work inhibiting missionary activity and limiting its exercise. Crucial as it is, "missionary activity," the Pope warns, which is "specifically directed 'to the nations' [*ad gentes*] appears to be waning." While there are indications of a "new springtime" for Christianity, the Pope notes "an undeniable negative tendency" in the area of mission. His encyclical was written to counter that tendency and invite the Church "to renew her missionary commitment" (2). In their pastoral statement on world mission, *To the Ends of the Earth*, the Catholic bishops of the United States did the same while addressing the more limited context of the United States: "We are faithful to the nature of the Church," they said, "to the degree that we love and sincerely promote her missionary activity" (2).

This book is the product of a symposium sponsored by the Committee on the Missions of the National Conference of Catholic Bishops in the United States. The purpose of the book, as it was of the symposium, is to explore some of the major theological and doctrinal issues treated in the encyclical, to situate these historically, particularly in relation to Vatican II, and to show their ramifications for the Church's mission *ad gentes*.

The book focuses on four major areas, including the relationship of the Church to the kingdom of God, the role of the Church in the work of salvation, the life and mission of the Church in relation to culture, and the place of dialogue in the missionary activity of the Church. Each of these areas has profound implications for the mission *ad gentes*. Some of the questions are theoretical, but even these have a very practical bearing on the exercise of mission.

The issues raised are a challenge for all, for those who are responsible for the mission of the Church, for theologians and all who are directly or indirectly involved in world mission. The position taken on these issues can contribute to the "new springtime" noted by John Paul II or accentuate the "undeniable negative tendency" which moved him to write the encyclical.

The four areas treated fall into two categories. The first, whose issues surround the Church's relationship to the kingdom of God and the work of salvation, focuses on the need and urgency of the universal mission. The basic question raised is very simple. Should the Church engage in the mission *ad gentes*?

The second category, whose issues involve the relationship of the Church to culture and the role of interreligious dialogue in missionary activity, has to do with the way of exercising missionary activity and with its effectiveness. Again the basic question raised is very simple. How can the Church best fulfill its mission *ad gentes*?

In a review of Vaclav Havel's *Open Letters, Selected Writings, 1965–1990* (New York: Knopf, 1991), Irving Howe observed that we turn to Vaclav Havel "not for theoretical innovation but for the consolidation of truth" (*The New York Times Book Review,* May 26, 1991, 5). It is in that same spirit that the presenters at the symposium prepared their papers and that they are offered in the following pages. To further that purpose, each paper is followed by a response prepared by another presenter, and an apt synthesis serves as a conclusion.

Pope John Paul devoted all of chapter 2 in his encyclical on mission to the kingdom of God, how Christ makes it present, its characteristics and demands, how it is fulfilled and proclaimed in the risen Christ, its relationship to Christ and the Church, and how the Church is at its service. In their pastoral statement, the bishops of the United States included a section on the kingdom in relation to the mission and person of Jesus as well as the nature of the Church and the way it continues Jesus' mission for the coming of the kingdom (24–26). In this book's opening chapter, Fr. Avery Dulles, S.J., preeminent among today's theologians for his efforts at the consolidation of theological truth, comes to grips with the "proliferation of new opinions about the kingdom of God," which is "one of the chief sources of confusion and conflict in contemporary missiology." Beginning with the biblical data and setting out the theological tradition, he sorts out the various issues related to the Church and the kingdom in relation to the *eschaton* and within history, critiques today's secularization theology, and examines recent papal teaching.

In his encyclical, Pope John Paul also devoted the whole of chapter 1 to the subject of Jesus Christ as the only Savior, painstakingly showing how this faith position is not a denial of human freedom, how the Church is a sign and instrument of salvation, and how the possibility of that salvation is offered to everyone. In their pastoral statement, the bishops of the United States underlined the importance of "the explicit proclamation of salvation in Jesus Christ" (27), showing how "mission is characterized . . . by a deep concern for the salvation of others and a profound respect for the ways they have already searched and experienced God" (32). In this book's second chapter, Archbishop J.

Francis Stafford brings a penetrating and analytical eye to the various contemporary issues surrounding the Church's mission of salvation. With special attention to the teaching of Vatican II, he addresses the vocation of the Catholic Church as a sacrament of God's saving will for all humankind, applies its saving mission to the Church in the United States, and draws out some pastoral implications as we prepare to celebrate the third millenium of the incarnation.

A major issue treated by Pope John Paul in his encyclical was that of culture and inculturation, which was taken up in chapter 5 as one of the paths of mission (52–54). The Pope presented the process of inculturation as a lengthy and difficult one through which "the Church makes the Gospel incarnate in different cultures and at the same time introduces peoples, together with their cultures, into her own community" (52). In their pastoral statement, the bishops of the United States spoke of the Church as "a leaven for all cultures, at home in each culture" (44). They presented true inculturation as occurring "when the Gospel penetrates the heart of cultural experience and shows how Christ gives new meaning to authentic human values" (44). In the third chapter of this book, Bishop Francis George, O.M.I., speaks authoritatively from a long experience of both the mission world and cultural anthropology. After situating the issue of Church and cultures in recent magisterial teaching, he takes up the various questions involved in the "inculturation of the faith" and "the evangelization of culture" and shows how these are related to the process of missionary evangelization.

In the fifth chapter of his encyclical, Pope John Paul also took up the question of "dialogue with our brothers and sisters of other religions." He presented interreligious dialogue as a part of the Church's evangelizing mission which enriches the mission efforts of the Church so long as it is conducted out of firm faith commitment and with docility to the Holy Spirit (55–57). In their pastoral statement on world mission, the bishops of the United States also dealt with mission and dialogue (40–44). They spoke of the role of dialogue as a "vital characteristic of mission," while not being "the goal of missionary proclamation," which is conversion (42). In this book's fourth chapter, J. Augustine DiNoia, O.P., brings his theological scalpel to bear in defining the present contours of the mission and dialogue problematic in which the commitment to both mission and dialogue is difficult to reconcile theologically. He then suggests a doctrinal resolution for the post-Vatican II missionary context.

In conclusion, I make mine the hopes expressed by Sr. Joan Gormley, S.S.M.W., in her concluding reflective synthesis. I pray "that the Lord will accomplish in us something of what he accomplished in the many Christians who were missionaries before us and that he will raise up many willing to give their very lives in order that all might know the unsearchable riches of Christ Jesus and be transformed in the light of his face."

Eugene LaVerdiere, S.S.S.
March 1, 1992

I

The Church and the Kingdom

Avery Dulles, S.J.

One of the chief sources of confusion and conflict in contemporary missiology is the proliferation of new opinions about the kingdom of God, which some authors understand as virtually identical with the Church while others look on it as separable from the Church and even from Christ. In order to bring some light on this debatable question I propose to examine, first of all, the biblical data concerning the kingdom and its relationship to the Church. I shall then consider the same relationships in the Catholic theological tradition and in the current teaching of the magisterium, and finally draw some conclusions.

1) The Kingdom: Biblical Data

The term "kingdom of God" is a biblical metaphor used in the Gospels with connotations derived both from Jewish apocalyptic literature and from rabbinic teaching. In the apocalyptic tradition it generally denotes a sudden, catastrophic event produced by God alone, introducing a radically new order and putting an end to history as we know it. The rabbis, for their part, tend to understand the kingdom as a divinely willed order realized in some degree within history through the faithful observance of the Torah. Some rabbinic texts connect the kingdom with the advent of the Messiah and the restoration of Israel as a political power. Although these pre-Christian traditions are not determinative for the New Testament, they give valuable background for understanding the ways in which Jesus and his contemporaries speak of the kingdom.

The theme of the "kingdom," which is central to the proclamation of John the Baptist and Jesus, takes on a specifically Christian meaning in light of the person and mission of Jesus.[1] This meaning, however, is very flexible. In the Gospels it seems to include any or all of the eschatological blessings, especially those manifestly brought about through Jesus the Messiah. After the resurrection the metaphor of the kingdom recedes to a secondary position in Christian discourse. The primary content of Christian proclamation is no longer the kingdom but rather Jesus Christ, in whom the kingdom of God is dynamically present. In proclaiming Christ, the Church is announcing the kingdom in a new way, for it is in and through him that God chooses to reign. Christ is often called King or Lord.

The term *basileia* in the Greek New Testament frequently means kingship (reign) but it sometimes must be translated as kingdom (realm). The two concepts are inseparable. Christ's kingship or lordship implies a community over which he reigns—in other words, a kingdom. Conversely, the concept of the kingdom always implies a king. Several different expressions such as "kingdom of God," "kingdom of heaven," "kingdom of the Son," and "kingdom of Christ" are used almost interchangeably in the New Testament, and the differences of nuance among them need not concern us here.

On the basis of the New Testament texts, theologians have concocted a variety of theories about the relationship between the kingdom and historical time. Some prefer to reserve the term "kingdom" for the final eschatological reality achieved when Christ "hands over the kingdom to his God and Father, when he has destroyed every sovereignty and every authority and power" (1 Cor 15:24). This purely futurist interpretation, while supported by some texts, runs into conflict with others that refer to the kingdom as something that has already broken into the world in the ministry of Jesus. For example, Jesus himself is reported as saying: "If it is by the finger of God that [I] drive out demons, then the kingdom of God has come upon you" (Luke 11:20; see Matt 12:28). After his resurrection Christ enters into the fullness of his kingdom and sends forth his Spirit upon the community of the disciples, which becomes a zone where he

---

1. The literature on the idea of the kingdom of God in the Gospels is too vast to be surveyed here. Several books may be listed as particularly useful for the present project: Rudolf Schnackenburg, *God's Rule and Kingdom* (New York: Herder and Herder, 1963); Norman Perrin, *Jesus and the Language of the Kingdom* (Philadelphia: Fortress, 1976); Jean Carmignac, *Le Mirage de l'Eschatologie: Royauté, Règne et Royaume de Dieu . . . sans Eschatologie* (Paris: Letouzey et Ané, 1979); and Bruce Chilton, ed., *The Kingdom of God in the Teaching of Jesus* (Philadelphia: Fortress, 1984).

reigns in a special way. On the basis of this rich array of texts most theologians hold that the kingdom exists not only in heaven or in the eschatological future but also, in an imperfect way, within time on earth. It was present incipiently in the public ministry of Jesus and continues to be present in the Christian community since the resurrection. The kingdom will come into its definitive phase in the age to come.

2) The Church and the Final Kingdom

Biblical Data. How, then, is the Church related to the kingdom of God? The New Testament does not afford materials for a full answer to this question because the kingdom appears chiefly in the Gospels, in which the Church is rarely mentioned, and because the Church is dealt with in other biblical books that say little about the kingdom.

So far as I am aware, there is only one text in which Church and kingdom are mentioned together: "And so I say to you, you are Peter, and upon this rock I will build my church, and the gates of the netherworld shall not prevail against it. I will give you the keys to the kingdom of heaven. Whatever you bind on earth shall be bound in heaven; and whatever you loose on earth shall be loosed in heaven" (Matt 16:18-19). Peter, by the same act, is made the foundation of the Church of Christ and the keeper of the keys of the kingdom of heaven. The metaphor of binding and loosing reappears in Matthew 18:18: "Whatever you bind on earth shall be bound in heaven, and whatever you loose on earth shall be loosed in heaven." "Heaven" in the second quotation may be equivalent to the "kingdom of Heaven" in the first. In both texts the correct interpretation may well be that decisions made in the Church on earth have validity for a person's definitive participation in the ultimate kingdom.

Some theologians write as though the Church were a purely human organization existing before the parousia, whereas the kingdom, they would say, is an eschatological reality to be consummated at the end of time. Wolfhart Pannenberg, for instance, writes: "Certainly the Kingdom of God is not the Church. Indeed it is quite possible to conceive of the Kingdom of God without any Church at all. The Kingdom of God is that perfect society of men which is to be realized in history by God himself. In Revelation, Saint John the Divine envisions such a society in which there is no need for church or temple. . . . Christ points the Church toward the Kingdom of God that is beyond the Church."[2]

Hans Küng, while he recognizes that the reign of God is already effective in the Church, maintains that according to modern exegesis it is impossible to speak of the Church as being God's kingdom on earth or the present form of the kingdom of God. It is important, in Küng's view, to stress the basic difference between the Church and the kingdom. To apply to the Church what is said in the New Testament about the reign of God will, he fears, lead to an ecclesiology of glory with the Church as its goal. In a series of contrasts between the Church and the kingdom, Küng declares that the Church grows from below and that it is definitely the work of human beings. The kingdom, however, comes from above and is definitely the work of God. "*Ekklesia*," he writes, "is a pilgrimage through the interim period of the last days, something provisional; *basileia* is the final glory at the end of all time, something definitive."[3]

These quotations from Pannenberg and Küng, in my judgment, exaggerate the contrast, particularly with regard to the Church, which they understand too narrowly as a this-worldly entity, produced by human effort, and destined for extinction at the end of time. This view should be challenged both exegetically and theologically. The *ekklesia* of the New Testament is a predominantly eschatological reality, given from above. It is the equivalent of what the Old Testament describes as "the assembly of the saints of the Most High" (Dan 7:27). That assembly will become complete when Christ returns in glory, bringing the faithful into their promised inheritance. The Church is likewise described in terms of metaphors such as the temple that is being built, the body that is growing up into unity with Christ its head, the new Jerusalem that descends from heaven, and the bride adorned for the wedding. None of these images suggests that the Church is destined to be abolished at the end of time. On the contrary, they imply that the Church on earth is merely the initial phase of the consummated, heavenly Church. The glorious consummation described in Revelation, chapter 21, to which Pannenberg alludes in the passage I have quoted, far from doing away with the Church, establishes it as the new Jerusalem, a city built upon the foundation of the twelve apostles (Rev

2. Wolfhart Pannenberg, *Theology and the Kingdom of God* (Philadelphia: Westminster, 1969) 76–77.

3. Hans Küng, *The Church* (New York: Sheed & Ward, 1968) 92–93; quotation from 93.

21:12-14). If the city contains no temple, that is because the entire city is a holy reality, suffused with God's transfiguring presence.

Theological Tradition. Throughout the patristic and medieval periods it was generally agreed that, although the Church is currently in a state of pilgrimage, it will come into its own in splendor at the end of time.[4] This eschatological dimension was somewhat lost to view after the Reformation. Almost absent from the theology of the nineteenth century, it was recovered in a number of statements, particularly by Protestants in the World Council of Churches after 1948. The final report of the Lund Conference of Faith and Order, held in 1952, and the Faith and Order Report received by the Evanston Assembly in 1954 both affirmed that the perfect unity of the Church will be achieved only when the glorious Christ returns to meet his Church.

In Catholic teaching this eschatological renewal of ecclesiology was accomplished, or at least officially endorsed, by Vatican II. The Dogmatic Constitution on the Church, in article 2, asserts that the Church "will achieve its glorious completion at the end of the ages," when all the just are gathered together in the universal Church in the presence of the Father. Article 5 states that the Church on earth, still growing, "hopes and desires with all its strength to be joined in glory with its king." Article 48 clearly affirms that the Church "will attain its consummation only in the glory of heaven." It also says that the Church on earth is a universal sacrament of the salvation that is to come, and that the sacraments and institutions of the Church pertain only to this present time. Article 51 states that when Christ appears, "the whole Church of the saints in the supreme happiness of love will adore God and 'the lamb who was slain' (Rev 5:12)."

If one looks on both the kingdom and the Church as existing proleptically within history and definitively at the close of history, it becomes more difficult to see how they differ. With regard to the final phase it must be asked: Is the consummation of the Church something different from the definitive arrival of the kingdom of God? The Pastoral Constitution on the Church in the Modern World makes the point in article 39 that "all the good fruits of our nature and enterprise produced on earth in the Spirit of the Lord and in accord with his command" will be found again, in a purified and transfigured form, in

---

4. In this paragraph I summarize material presented at greater length in my article, "The Church as Eschatological Community," in Joseph Papin, ed., *The Eschaton: A Community of Love* (Villanova, Pa.: Villanova University Press, 1971) 69–103.

the final kingdom. This text seems to imply that the world itself, in all its secularity, will be transformed in Christ. It then becomes very difficult to distinguish between the glorified Church and the transformed cosmos. Perhaps one should say that the heavenly Church, as the place where Christ rules in the assembly of the saints, will be at the heart and center of the ultimate kingdom. The new heavens and the new earth, while they may include more than the transfigured Church, will serve to mediate and express the blessed life of the redeemed.

3) Church and Kingdom within History

Biblical Data. More complex is the question of the relationship between the Church and the kingdom within history. As I have mentioned, it is difficult to settle this problem from the New Testament. In the famous Petrine text from Matthew, quoted above, there is evidently a very close relationship, and some would say an identity, between the Church founded on Peter and the kingdom to which Peter receives the keys. In many other passages what is said about the kingdom can easily be interpreted as referring to the Church. For instance Jesus, as reported by Luke, says that "the law and the prophets lasted until John; but from then on the kingdom of God is proclaimed" (Luke 16:16). Even the least in the kingdom of heaven is greater than John (Matt 11:11). Then again, Jesus consoles the "little flock" of his disciples because it has pleased the Father to give them the kingdom (Luke 12:32). According to the Fourth Gospel, Jesus teaches the necessity of being reborn by water and the Holy Spirit in order to enter the kingdom of God (John 3:3-5). This could be understood as entrance into the Church through baptism.

The Letter to the Colossians speaks of Christians as having been rescued from the power of darkness and transferred into the kingdom of God's beloved Son (Col 1:13). The Book of Revelation speaks of those ransomed by the blood of Christ as having been made "a kingdom and priests for our God" (Rev 5:10; see 1:6). In many of these texts the term "Church" could be substituted for "kingdom" without any evident change of meaning.

The parables of the kingdom in the Synoptic Gospels bring us into the very difficult area of parable interpretation. Many critics hold today that the kingdom must here be interpreted as a poetic metaphor with various levels of meaning. Even so, however, one level of meaning would seem to refer to the Church. These parables speak of a reality that begins as a small seed, undergoes astonishing growth, and is to be harvested at the end of time. The kingdom, as presented in these parables, seems to encompass both the righteous and sinners, who will be separated from one another at the final judgment. All these attributes of the kingdom fit the Church. Speaking of Matthew's vision of the Church, the New Testament exegete John R. Donahue writes: "The Church is a *corpus mixtum*, a body in which the good and the bad are mixed together. Like the mustard seed, it is small and insignificant, but it will become a tree. Its growth is as imperceptible as that of the rising of leavened bread. . . . Therefore, in these parables, which along with the Sower are addressed to the crowds (= potential believers in Matthew's own day), Matthew explains the paradoxical nature of the Church."[5]

Some competent scholars continue to maintain that the Church in the New Testament is identical with the kingdom of God.[6] For a variety of reasons this opinion, in my judgment, is somewhat excessive. The kingdom, as I have said, is sometimes identified with the work of Christ in his public ministry, even prior to the founding of the Church. At other times, the kingdom is treated as a future eschatological reality. Even after the Church is established, Christians still have to pray for the coming of the kingdom, as we do in the "Our Father." Then again, Jesus indicates that the kingdom will be taken away from the Jews (Matt 21:43), but the Jews never possessed the Church. Furthermore, metaphors such as the hidden treasure and the pearl of great price (Matt 7:44-46), which are depicted as standing for the kingdom, are difficult to apply to the Church. For the New Testament, then, one may conclude that, while many kingdom sayings can be applied to the Church, the kingdom and the Church do not seem totally to coincide.

Theological Tradition. Origen in his commentary on Matthew asserts that Christ, because he is God's wisdom, righteousness, and truth, is the kingdom itself (*autobasileia*).[7] In the West, where the concept of the kingdom was more fully developed, theologians were inclined to link the kingdom of God more closely with the Church.

Augustine is often considered the principal proponent of the thesis

---

5. John R. Donahue, *The Gospel in Parable* (Philadelphia: Fortress, 1988) 67–68.

6. This is the conclusion of Jean Carmignac in *Le mirage de l'eschatologie*, especially 95–102.

7. Origen, *In Matt.* 14:7 (GCS 40:289).

that the Church and the kingdom of God are one and the same thing, but his language is not consistent. In a number of sermons and in an important passage from the *City of God* (book 20, chapter 9), he aligns the city of God with the Church and the earthly city with the state, especially in its evil aspects, where the state is seen as demonic. But Augustine recognizes that the Church in its present form contains an admixture of evil, and that it will not be perfected until Christ's return in glory. Gregory the Great, simplifying somewhat the thought of Augustine, states that "in Holy Scripture the Church of the present time is frequently called the Kingdom of Heaven."[8] Medieval theologians such as Hugh of St. Victor identify Augustine's two cities respectively with the spiritual power (the Church) and the secular power (the Empire).

Thomas Aquinas in his *Commentary on the Sentences* holds that to be in the kingdom is to be perfectly subjected to God's providence, which orders us to our last end. He then continues: "The Kingdom of God antonomastically signifies two things: sometimes the assembly (*congregatio*) of those who are journeying in faith, and in that case it is the Church militant that is the Kingdom of God; at other times, the communion (*collegium*) of those who are established in the end, and then it is the Church triumphant that is the Kingdom of God."[9] In the *Summa theologiae* Thomas does not make a direct comparison between the two terms, but he seems to ascribe the same attributes to both. At one point, when discussing the kingdom of God, Thomas maintains that Christ's rule is exercised predominantly through obedience to the inner law of grace (1-2.108.1 *ad* 1). At another point he declares that the Church as body of Christ is constituted primarily by the grace of Christ the head that flows into the members (3.8.6c). Thus St. Thomas tends to spiritualize both Church and kingdom and to see them as very similar, if not identical.

The idea of the kingdom of God has undergone many transformations in Protestant theology. Martin Luther, influenced by Augustine, drew a sharp contrast between the kingdom of God and the kingdom of the world, but he saw the two as dialectically intertwined, inasmuch as God rules to some degree through worldly governments. Many Lutherans and Pietists understood the kingdom of God as a matter of interior faith and devotion, unrelated to public affairs, which belonged to the worldly regime. Liberal Protestants such as Albert

---

8. *Homilies on the Gospels*, Bk. I, hom. 17, no. 1 (ML 76:1118); see his *Moralia*, Bk. 33, chap. 18, no. 34 (CC 143B:1704).

9. *In IV Sent.*, Dist. 49, qu. 1, art. 2, q'la 5, sol. 5 (Paris: Vives, 11:470).

Ritschl and Adolf Harnack situated the kingdom of God initially in the hearts of individuals, and looked for its completion in the organization of humanity through actions inspired by love. In Walter Rauschenbusch and other proponents of the "social gospel" the Puritans' expectation of the kingdom was blended with democratic ideals. The kingdom came to be seen, to a large extent, as a just and prosperous society brought about through Christian activism. At the end of the nineteenth century Albert Schweitzer and others rediscovered the apocalyptic features of Jesus' teaching concerning the kingdom.

In the documents of the Catholic magisterium the kingdom is frequently depicted as in some respects transcending the Church. Pope Pius XI reflected on the relationship in several of his encyclicals. In *Ubi arcano* (1922) he chose as the motto of his pontificate, "The peace of Christ in the kingdom of Christ." In 1925 he published the encyclical *Quas primas* on Christ the King. In both these encyclicals he pointed out that Christ's empire is all-encompassing; it includes the secular as well as the religious, the temporal as well as the spiritual, the natural as well as the supernatural. The Church, on the other hand, has a limited sphere of authority. Although the Church has the mandate to proclaim to all peoples the law of God in matters of faith and morals, it lacks competence in merely secular affairs and has no direct power over secular rulers. According to Pius XI, therefore, the reign of Christ is not restricted to the Church.

Vatican II handled the question very cautiously. The Dogmatic Constitution on the Church speaks of the Church on earth as "the Kingdom of Christ already present in mystery" (3). It also states that the Church has "the mission of announcing the Kingdom of Christ and of God and of inaugurating it among all peoples," for the Church is "the seed and beginning of the Kingdom upon earth" (5). The Decree on the Church's Missionary Activity, after repeating this point, adds that it is the task of the Church to "spread to all parts of the world the Kingdom of Christ" and thus prepare for his coming (1). These texts can certainly be read as suggesting that the Church alone is the seed of the kingdom, and that any extension of the kingdom is an extension of the Church, but they do not need to be read in this way. The Pastoral Constitution on the Church in the Modern World, after declaring that all the values of human dignity, fellowship, and freedom realized in human society will be found eminently in the final kingdom, remarks that the kingdom itself is mysteriously present here on earth (39). The implication would seem to be that the kingdom is mysteriously present in secular society, since the values men-

4) Secularization Theology

Richard McBrien, in a book published shortly after Vatican II,[10] notes that some of the council's statements could be read in either of two ways. According to the first reading, which he calls Ptolemaic, the Church is simply identified with the kingdom. According to the second reading, which McBrien calls Copernican, the kingdom of God, not the Church, must be regarded as central. The astronomical analogy seems to imply that the Church revolves about the kingdom like a satellite or planet around the sun. According to this "Copernican" view, which McBrien regards as biblically and theologically correct, the Church exists for the sake of the kingdom, of which it is a sign and instrument. The Church, he says, is "one of the principal agents whereby the human community is made to stand under the judgment of the enduring values of the Gospel of Jesus Christ: freedom, justice, peace, charity, compassion, reconciliation" (229). All are called to the kingdom, he holds, but only some are called to the Church. "Salvation," he writes, "comes through participation in the Kingdom of God rather than through affiliation with the Christian Church" (228). In McBrien's estimation Vatican II, in clinging to elements of the Ptolemaic vision, set itself somewhat at odds with reality, and was far less radical than it ought to have been (165).

McBrien's *Do We Need the Church?*, from which these quotations are drawn, is only one of a number of books that came out in the 1960s representing secularization theology. In this movement a sharp contrast was made between the Church and the kingdom of God. What was finally important was not anything specific to the Church, such as faith or worship, but a set of abstract human values that could be accepted by any person of good will: freedom, peace, justice, and friendship. The mission of the Church—if it is legitimate to speak of mission at all—was to get people involved in the building of a better human society, along the lines of Harvey Cox's "secular city." This ideal society came to be dignified with the title "kingdom of God." It was unimportant whether people believed in Christ, except insofar as belief in Christ might motivate them to work more assiduously for the reconstruction of secular society. In some cases the traditional concept

---

10. *Do We Need the Church?* (New York: Harper & Row, 1969).

of mission was practically inverted. According to a formula that enjoyed wide currency in the World Council of Churches, the world should set the agenda for the Church.[11]

A sharp distinction between Church and kingdom is characteristic also of much Latin American liberation theology. An expert in this field, after asserting that "The Church is not the kingdom; it is to serve the kingdom," goes on to say: "That dictum is a kind of first principle of Latin American ecclesiology. . . . The kingdom is a situation in which people can live together as brothers and sisters. . . . The practical pastoral application is that the church finds its raison d'être not in itself but in the community it is to serve. . . . In this context the service of the church consists of 'the ongoing humanization of the human realm at every level and in every situation.'"[12]

This secular or liberationist theology of the kingdom has had an enormous impact on recent theologies of missionary activity, the theme of the conference for which this paper was written. Paul Knitter, in his influential book, *No Other Name?*, calls for "a thorough overhauling of the traditional model of missionary work." Such an overhauling is now possible, he holds, because of recent advances in the theology of the kingdom:

> Christian theology, both Protestant and Catholic, admits that the church is not to be identified with God's kingdom. The kingdom, God's revealing-saving presence in the world, is much broader than the church and also operates through means other than the church. The primary mission of the church, therefore, is not the "salvation business" (making persons Christian so that they can be saved), but the task of serving and promoting the kingdom of justice and love, by being sign and servant, wherever that kingdom may be forming.[13]

Although the secular, kingdom-centered theology of authors such as Pannenberg, McBrien, Berryman, and Knitter has many eager adherents, its deficiencies have been pointed out by other scholars. Jacques Dupuis, after conceding that the kingdom is broader than the Church, argues persuasively that "the Kingdom of God is necessarily

---

11. See Walter J. Hollenweger, ed., *The Church for Others* (Geneva: World Council of Churches, 1967).

12. Philip Berryman, *Liberation Theology* (Oak Park, Ill.: Meyer, Stone Books, 1987) 158–60. The final quotation is from Jon Sobrino.

13. Paul F. Knitter, *No Other Name?* (Maryknoll, N.Y.: Orbis, 1985) 222.

Christic in both its dimensions, the historical and the eschatological, the 'already' and the 'not yet.'"[14]

5) Recent Papal Teaching

The recent popes have emphasized that the kingdom of God is an essentially religious concept, and that it cannot be separated either from Christ or from the Church. Paul VI, in his apostolic exhortation *On Evangelization in the Modern World* (1975) wrote that the Church "reaffirms the primacy of her spiritual vocation and refuses to replace the proclamation of the Kingdom by the proclamation of forms of human liberation; she even states that her contribution to liberation is incomplete if she neglects to proclaim salvation in Jesus Christ" (34).

Early in his pontificate, at Puebla in January 1979, John Paul II quoted his predecessor, John Paul I, as saying: "It is wrong to state that political, economic, and social liberation coincides with salvation, that the *regnum Dei* (kingdom of God) is identified with the *regnum hominis* (kingdom of man)." Speaking for himself, John Paul II went on to deplore "the separation which some set up between the church and the kingdom of God. The kingdom of God is emptied of its full content and is understood in a rather secularist sense: It is interpreted as being reached not by faith and membership in the church but by the mere changing of structures and social and political involvement, and as being present whenever there is a certain type of involvement and activity for justice."[15]

A more formal and complete statement on the nature of the kingdom and its relation to the Church's mission may be found in chapter 2 of John Paul II's recent encyclical, *Redemptoris missio* (On the Permanent Validity of the Church's Missionary Mandate, December 7, 1990). The kingdom of God, he says, "is the manifestation and the realization of God's plan of salvation in all its fullness" (15). In the preaching of the early Church, the kingdom was rightly identified with Christ (16). The kingdom of God, as we know it from revelation, "is not a concept, a doctrine or a program subject to free interpretation, but is before all else a person with the face and name of Jesus of Nazareth" (18). To proclaim the kingdom, therefore, is to proclaim

---

14. Jacques Dupuis, "The Kingdom of God and World Religions," *Vidyajyoti: Journal of Theological Reflection* 51 (1987) 530–44.

15. "Pope John Paul's Address at Puebla," *Origins* 8 (February 8, 1979) 529–38, quotation from 532.

Christ and the gospel. The kingdom, which was already present in the person of Jesus during his public ministry, is slowly being established in the world as people enter into a mysterious communion with Jesus (16).

This vision of the kingdom is sharply opposed to the reductionistic visions proposed in secularization theology. In anthropocentric thinking, says the Pope, "the kingdom tends to become something completely human and secularized" (17). Such a view, though it points out certain genuine values that should not be overlooked, "easily translates into one more ideology of earthly progress" (17). In particular, the Pope repudiates conceptions that describe themselves as "kingdom centered" rather than ecclesiocentric. According to these authors, John Paul remarks, the Church must be the "church for others" and promote values such as peace, justice, freedom, and brotherhood, rather than anything distinctively Christian. I have already given several examples of what the Pope seems to have in mind.

The kingdom of God, according to John Paul II, is not simply the kingdom of man. Christ's kingdom is "not of this world" (17; cf. John 18:36). To bypass Christ and redemption is to denature the kingdom. The kingdom in its fullness requires authentic values grounded in the mystery of creation (17–18), but above and beyond these human values it includes others that are properly evangelical, since they derive from Christ and the gospel (19). Because these latter values are essential, "entry into the kingdom comes through faith and conversion" (13). The Gospels, which attest to this, teach also that "the kingdom will grow insofar as every person learns to turn to God in the intimacy of prayer as to a Father . . . and strives to do his will" (13).

These reflections prepare for what the Pope has to say about the relation between the kingdom of God and the Church. The kingdom cannot be detached from the Church any more than it can be detached from Christ, for Christ has endowed the Church, his body, with the fullness of the blessings and means of salvation (18). The Church has a specific and necessary role in the process of salvation, for it is commissioned to announce and to inaugurate the kingdom among all peoples (18).

The present pope is willing to say, as did Paul VI, that the Church is at the service of the kingdom (20). But he makes it clear that this service is accomplished first of all in the proclamation of the gospel. "Proclamation," he says, "is the permanent priority of mission. . . . All forms of missionary activity are directed to this proclamation, which reveals and give access to the mystery hidden for ages and made known in Christ" (44). The Church serves the kingdom preeminently "by establishing communities and founding new particular churches and by guiding them to mature faith and charity" (20).

The Pope does not minimize the value of "human promotion, commitment to justice and peace, education and the care of the sick, and aid to the poor and to children" (20). These concerns, as the Pope says, pertain to God's kingdom; they legitimately enter into the Church's task as she labors to assist humanity on its journey toward the eschatological kingdom. But in carrying on these activities, the Pope concludes, the Church "never loses sight of the priority of the transcendent and spiritual realities which are premises of eschatological salvation" (20). The "temporal dimension of the kingdom remains incomplete unless it is related to the kingdom of Christ present in the Church and straining toward eschatological fullness" (20).

6) Conclusion

Because the Holy Father has so fully and lucidly addressed the questions before us in his recent encyclical, a very brief concluding reflection may suffice. The task of the Church's missionary activity is evangelization. Evangelization may be taken either in a narrow or in a broad sense of the word. In the narrow sense it means an initial proclamation of the gospel to individuals or groups that do not as yet believe in Christ, with a view of making them believers. In a broad sense evangelization includes the task of bringing the values of the gospel into every area of human life, so as to transform humanity, renew it in Christ, and prepare it for the life to come.[16]

Evangelizing in both these senses, the missionary serves the kingdom of God. The full service of the kingdom includes the promotion of all those human values that stem from the order of creation and pertain directly or indirectly to the Christian life. Labor for peace, justice, and the alleviation of misery should not be seen as alien to the missionary task. But it will be understood that full acceptance of the social implications of Christianity cannot be achieved without faith in the gospel. Because Jesus Christ himself is the core and summit of the kingdom, and the transcendent source of all authentically Christian values, missionaries must be primarily concerned with spreading the knowledge and love of Christ. Where the name of Christ is not proclaimed, the heralding of the kingdom is seriously deficient. Where

---

16. On the nature of missionary evangelization, see the Vatican paper, "Dialogue and Proclamation," *Origins* 21 (July 4, 1991) 121–35.

prayer and worship are not practiced, the kingdom of God is not sought as it should be.

Something of the Church is present, no doubt, wherever the Holy Spirit is at work and wherever the values of the gospel are honored. Strictly speaking, however, the Church on earth must be more narrowly understood as the divinely established, visible community of men and women who believe in Christ. That community is not the totality of the kingdom of God; it must seek to serve the kingdom in all its phases and dimensions. In describing such service one must take care not to give the impression that the Church is a mere means for achieving some higher goal outside itself. The Church, as the body of Christ, is not subordinate to any created reality except the sacred humanity of Christ our Lord. In the eyes of believers, it should be obvious that the kingdom of God cannot be adequately realized apart from the Church. Missionary activity, in seeking to achieve an inner conversion of hearts and minds to Christ the King, serves the Church. Successfully evangelized Christians will place a high value on faith and on the Church's "sacred" activities of prayer and worship. But precisely because of their commitment to Christ and the Church, they will also strive to promote "secular" values such as justice, peace, and love among all human beings, both within the Church and beyond its visible borders.

Response

Francis E. George, O.M.I.

With customary clarity, Father Dulles has taken us through the sources in order to assess the relationship between kingdom and Church, both at the *eschaton* and now, within history, and has then adjudicated a conclusion which does justice to the various claims and enables us to move on with enlightened faith and heartened spirit. We all have reason, once again, to be grateful to him.

Quoting number 48 of *Lumen gentium*, the Dogmatic Constitution on the Church, Father Dulles calls the Church a sacrament. We are also reminded that the Church is a sort of sacrament when Father

Dulles speaks of the Church as a visible community. I would therefore like to bring to this discussion of the relationship between kingdom and Church the suggestion that the relationship can be better understood by considering it as an analogue of the relation of *sacramentum* to *res*. The Church is the visible presence of a divine mystery, a mystery of faith which would remain invisible without her. The mystery, of course, is that of universal salvation, that is, the mystery of the kingdom of God, in which all are one with the Father, through Christ, in the Holy Spirit. In the kingdom, all are holy.

As visible, sacramental sign of this kingdom, the Church both discloses its presence and, in some way, also causes the kingdom to be present, to come. To borrow terminology from another discussion, the Church makes the eschatological kingdom realized now. The analogy falters, of course, when we ask what particular action of Christ is made present in the sacramental symbol. While "mission" might be an arguable analogue here, the lack of an immediate response indicates that the Church is not a "sacrament" like one of the seven sacraments.

The analogy is accurate enough, however, to prompt us to ask: what is there about the Church that enables us to call her the sacrament of the kingdom of God? What of her nature or structure makes her a sign of an invisible, transcendent, eschatological reign? On September 18, 1991, at the weekly general audience in Rome, Pope John Paul II commented on the parable of the wedding feast in Matthew 22. A wedding feast is a feast of love. The kingdom is like a wedding feast because the kingdom is a loving communion, a banquet given by the Father, at which Christ is bridegroom and, according to the Pope's use of Scripture at the general audience, the Church is bride. The Church sets the table of the Eucharist to unite herself continuously to her loving bridegroom until he returns in glory.

In December 1990, the Pope said all this in slightly less poetic fashion in *Redemptoris missio*, his encyclical On the Permanent Validity of the Church's Missionary Mandate. As Father Dulles has pointed out, the mission encyclical asserts that the kingdom of God is identified with a person, Jesus Christ, and entry into that kingdom is through communion, a particular kind of loving relationship, with Christ. The Church, then, is sacrament of the kingdom, because like the kingdom she is now a loving communion of persons; but, unlike the kingdom, she is not perfectly that loving communion.

The sea-change in ecclesiology approved by Vatican II is not a passage from "hierarchy" to "people." Both of these are societal metaphors and each is needed; but the radical difference in ecclesial self-understanding is the shift from society to communion in explaining what the Church is most fundamentally. In *Lumen gentium*, Vatican II draws upon Trinitarian theology to describe the Church as a communion of persons, as is the Godhead, and, in *Gaudium et spes*, explains that the relation between Church and world develops from the unique service which a loving communion of persons offers to a functionalist society. This service is one of humanizing, unifying, and sanctifying a human race now organized functionally and divided by conflicts of interest, by hatreds and injustices of various sorts. She transforms even the so-called "secular" values mentioned by Father Dulles; if defined as values of the kingdom, justice and peace take on meaning different from that which they enjoy in United States law or in modern society.

The contrast between communion and society is not fully defined in the council documents. To understand the contrast, we can think of the distinction in Weberian sociology between *Gemeinschaft* and *Gesellschaft*; but neither of these sets of relations speaks of transcendence, as does communion. We can also look at Aquinas's distinction, in a unity of order, between relations which unite members reciprocally, among themselves, and those which relate all members to a common good.

Another entree into a deeper understanding of these two sorts of relations—the one sort characterizing communion and, therefore, the kingdom of God, and the other sort characterizing society—is given us in the philosophical anthropology of Karol Wojtyla, whose interventions at the Second Vatican Council helped shape *Gaudium et spes*, the Pastoral Constitution on the Church in the Modern World. In Wojtyla's anthropological theory, when human subjects participate in common action, they relate in two ways. First, they relate as "I-You," the sort of relationship that arises when two subjects discover their respective subjectivity in experiencing the other simultaneously as object (You) and as other subject (I). The "I-You" relationship is characteristic of a community in which interpersonal relationship, unity, is its own goal. Marriage is a case in point. Second, subjects participating in common action can relate as "We," in a relationship which arises when two subjects only indirectly face each other while both act together for a common goal, the attainment of which leaves their personal differences more strongly experienced than their unity. A community becoming a communion of persons, a truly uniting community, will be constituted more by relationships of the "I-You" variety than by those of the "We" sort. A society, by contrast, will be characterized more by "We" relationships, expressive of its members striving for a common goal mostly external to their subjectivity.

In society, in the world, the Church is most clearly sacrament of the kingdom of God when she is most visibly, publicly, a unity formed by participation characterized by "I-You" relationships. Because the Church is also, in part, organized as a society, she will never be, until the end of history, perfectly a communion of persons. She will always in her life and action wrestle with the partial alienation which tells us that our existence is not fully Trinitarian, that participation in full communion is not yet realized; but the Church is in the world as servant of the kingdom to the extent that she is visibly a communion of persons open to God, to each other, and to the future, sharing the spiritual gifts bequeathed us by Christ and the material goods we have worked for ourselves. The secular analogue of ecclesial communion is human solidarity.

The mission of the Church is in service to the kingdom because she is the kingdom when her constitutive relationships anticipate and make present now the universal salvation willed by God. In *Redemptoris missio* (34), missionary activity incorporates (1) the work of proclaiming Christ and his gospel; (2) the work of building up the local Church; and (3) the work of promoting the values of Christ's kingdom. These values are those of communion: Trinitarian, spousal, ecclesial. The Church is faithful to her missionary vocation by being herself "the Kingdom of Christ already present in mystery" (*Lumen gentium* 3).

II

The Inscrutable Riches of Christ: The Catholic Church's Mission of Salvation

J. Francis Stafford, D.D.

During six weeks in 1956, my parents and I vacationed in Europe. We were together in the summer after my second year of theology at the North American College in Rome. Sometime in the course of those wonderful days, my father and I talked about the meaning of the priestly calling. At times, he said, it was difficult for him to understand my reasons for pursuing a vocation "in the Church." I had sensed for some time, in fact since 1952 when I entered Old St. Mary's on Paca Street in Baltimore, that my dad had held this question in his heart; but in the earliest days he probably thought it premature to ask. Now that ordination was only a summer away, he thought his question ripe for the asking.

My answer came spontaneously: "For the love of Christ," meaning that both Christ's love for me and my love for Christ were the source of a priestly vocation. I could not keep hidden within me "the inscrutable riches of Christ" (Eph 3:8). My father understood this response to come from depths which surprised us both, and he did not raise the question again during the twenty-eight years of life remaining to him on earth. I have never forgotten the occasion and have drawn upon the grace of that conversation many times since.

While reading Pope John Paul II's encyclical letter *Redemptoris missio* (RM), I recalled that summer day in central Italy. The Pope insistently asks, "Why mission?" And his most persuasive reply relies upon the Church's faith and experience of Christ.

> True liberation consists in opening oneself to the love of Christ. In him, and only in him, are we set free from all alienation and doubt, from

slavery to the power of sin and death. Christ is truly "our peace" (Eph 2:4); "the love of Christ impels us" (2 Cor 5:14), giving meaning and joy to our life. Mission is an issue of faith, an accurate indicator of our faith in Christ and his love for us (RM 11).

At bottom, the compelling motive for our missionary activity is the paschal mystery. Christ's passion, death, and resurrection are "for us" (*pro nobis*), as our creed proclaims, and "for me" (*pro me*), as St. Paul writes. The Son of God "has loved me and given himself up for me" (Gal 2:20).

I am certain that my confident, even surprisingly bold witness in conversation with my dad was the result of the work of the Holy Spirit in the Church. For it was the Church that called me each day to a free response to the love Christ freely gives in the Eucharist. It was the Church that unfolded for me the paschal mystery in the course of the liturgical year and on every Sunday. It was the Church that helped me discern the glory of God in the poor—really in all of creation. It was the Church that revealed that the whole world is a cosmic liturgy. To my dying day I cannot give sufficient thanks that the Church taught me the words of St. Francis of Assisi: "All praise be yours, my Lord, through all you have made . . . through my lord brother sun, . . . and through sister moon and stars."

I recall these events because they speak to me of the compelling nature of the Church's mission: "The love of Christ compels us!" (*Caritas Christi urget nos!*). Each of us must know this reality if we are to live out the Church's mission of salvation. Within this urgent call to love Christ, I will address the following three areas of concern: first, the vocation of the Catholic Church to be a sacrament of God's saving will for all humankind; second, the saving mission of the Catholic Church in the United States today; third, the Christian spirituality of the Second Vatican Council: *Lumen Christi*, the Light of Tabor, and its pastoral implications as we prepare for the celebration of the third millenium of the incarnation of the eternal Son of God.

1) The Catholic Church: Sacrament of God's Saving Will for All Humankind

The Church is the gathering in the Holy Spirit of the people called out of the world by God to proclaim in and to the world the mystery of Christ. From the beginning, the Father has gathered a people in whom and through whom he wishes to save every individual human being, and the gathering of the Church is inseparable from her mission to the world. Gathering and mission together belong to the essential nature of the Church. The Church is in mission, as are all Catholics, even if they are not explicitly aware of it: "We are missionaries above all because of what we are as a Church, whose inner life is unity in love even before we become missionaries in word and deed" (RM 23). Because of this "unity in love," the Church has been "sent by Christ to reveal and communicate the love of God to all peoples and nations" (*Ad gentes* 10).

Consequently, when Vatican II teaches that the Catholic Church is called to be the universal sacrament of salvation, the "to be" is not meant in the sense of becoming what the Church is not. The "unity in love" which is the Church and which the Catholic experiences, particularly in the celebration of the Eucharist, is a "share in the communion which exists between the Father and the Son" (RM 23). The Church is above all doxological, sacramental, Eucharistic, and covenantal. She cannot be reduced to a voluntary association. She is willed by God for the salvation of the human race. Unfortunately, the notion of Church as a voluntary society has been foundational for the religious experience of the American people since the Great Awakening.

At the conclusion of the Eucharistic Prayer, the priest with the people's "Amen" offers the great doxology to God the Almighty Father. It is from the Church in the unity of the Holy Spirit that all honor and glory arises through Christ, with Christ, and in Christ. The Church has been sent as a communion of life, love, and truth (*Lumen gentium* 9). In the fellowship of the Holy Spirit, who fills the universe, holds all things in unity, and knows everything that is said, the Church gathers together everything that, in this world, is for and tending toward God in a hymn of cosmic praise.

In the Nicene Creed, the Church confesses that "we believe in one Lord Jesus Christ." We confess the absolute, proper, and objective singularity of Jesus Christ. Vatican II repeatedly speaks of the unique position of Jesus Christ (GS 22; AG 8; SC 5, 83; LG 2, 8, 14, 27, 28, *passim*). Likewise John Paul II teaches, "It is precisely this uniqueness of Christ which gives him an absolute and universal significance, whereby, while belonging to history, he remains history's centre and goal" (RM 6). The predestination of Jesus Christ means that he is the One in whom all things were predestined and created (DS 536).

We believe with St. Irenaeus that "the invisible presence of the Logos has spread everywhere. . . . Through him, everything is under the redemptive economy, and the Son of God . . . has traced the sign of the cross on everything" (*Demonstration*, C 34). With St. Cyprian,

St. Hilary, and St. Augustine, we confess that the Word of God, from the very beginning and in every part of the world, gives a more or less obscure revelation of the Father to every creature.

But if every human being in all times and in every place can be saved through Christ, in principle at least and at whatever risk, what reason is there for the Church? How can it be claimed that the Church is still a vital necessity? What do these assertions about the absolute singularity of Jesus Christ imply concerning his Church, which the Second Vatican Council says is to be likened "by no mean analogy . . . to the mystery of the incarnate Word" (LG 8).

The Church is the one all-encompassing sacrament of salvation (LG 48). By Church is meant the unique Church of Christ which is the general means of salvation. It is through the Church that the fullness of the means of salvation can be obtained; and it is the Church which has been endowed with all divinely revealed truth and with all the means of salvation.[1] The council teaches clearly the full identity between the universal Church of Jesus Christ and the Roman Catholic Church. We read in *Orientalium ecclesiarum*, "The holy and Catholic Church . . . is the Mystical Body of Christ" (OE 2). The *Acta* on the Decree on Ecumenism states that this decree "clearly affirms that only the Catholic Church is the true Church of Christ."[2] In reflecting upon the documents of Vatican II, the *Acta*, and other magisterial documents, no other conclusion appears reasonable.

The Catholic Church is the "universal sacrament of salvation" (LG 48), based on a unique analogy between the incarnation and the Church. Just as the eternal Son of God assumed only one individual body for the ransom of humanity, so the Spirit of Christ through "the social structure" of the Catholic Church (*socialis compago*) is the organ of salvation for the world. Thus the Church develops a special pneumatic "life of its own in all the forms which are proper to it as a social structure in the Spirit."[3]

Cardinal Joseph Ratzinger finds in the documents of the Second Vatican Council the equation of the unique Church of Christ with the Roman Catholic Church.

---

1. See the 1973 instruction *Mysterium ecclesiae* of the Sacred Congregation for the Doctrine of the Faith (Washington: United States Catholic Conference, 1973).
2. *Acta Synodalia* 3, pt. 2, 12.
3. Aloys Grillmeier, "Dogmatic Constitution on the Church, Chapter I, The Mystery of the Church," in *Commentary on the Documents of Vatican II*, Herbert Vorgrimler, ed. (New York: Herder and Herder, 1967) 1:149.

[The] full concreteness of the Church does not mean that every other Church can only be a non-Church. The equation is not mathematical because the Holy Spirit cannot be reduced to a mathematical symbol, not even where he concretely binds and bestows himself. Mathematics is an abstraction even in the physical sphere but especially where there is question of God and man. Abstractions are clear, but one cannot build one's life on them. The working of the Holy Spirit is admittedly not clear, but it can be trusted: the equation is valid even though it cannot be stated mathematically.[4]

Fr. Francis Sullivan, S.J., of the Gregorian University believes otherwise. He writes that "one can think of the universal Church as a communion, at various levels of fullness, of bodies that are more or less fully Churches."[5] He concludes, therefore, that "there is one Church of God that embraces the particular Churches of both East and West."[6] Consequently, the Catholic Church, in his view, is one of many particular Churches. It appears that his position is in irreconcilable tension with two traditional doctrines: *extra Ecclesiam [Catholicam] nulla salus* ("no salvation outside the [Catholic] Church") and the coherence of the four marks of the Church.

With regard to the latter, Vatican II teaches, "This is the unique Church of Christ, which in the Creed we confess to be one, holy, catholic and apostolic" (LG 8). By reducing the Roman Catholic Church to the status of "a particular Church of the West," Sullivan neglects the teaching of *Lumen gentium* that the Church founded by Christ as a visible society and entrusted to Peter is the "unique Church of Christ"; he thereby places in eclipse, at least partially but really, one of the four essential properties of the universal Church that traditionally has been applied to the Roman Church, its catholicity. In my judgment, Sullivan's reduction of the Catholic Church to "a particular Church" affects the catholicity of the Church in a way unintended by and incompatible with the Decree on Ecumenism (4) precisely because it denies the uniqueness of the Catholic Church.

Fr. Anton Angel, S.J., also of the Gregorian University, states the issue in this way: "In the 'one Church—many churches' relationship,

---

4. Joseph Cardinal Ratzinger, *Principles of Catholic Theology* (San Francisco: Ignatius Press, 1987) 230–31.

5. Francis Sullivan, S.J., "The Significance of the Vatican II Declaration that the Church of Christ 'subsists in' the Roman Catholic Church," in *Vatican II: Assessment and Perspectives*, René Latourelle, ed. (New York: Paulist Press, 1989) 2:283.

6. Ibid.

one fact is very clear: Vatican II chose as a *point of departure* [emphasis in the original] the reality and idea of universal church or congregation of all the faithful in communion with the center, the supreme pastor and the whole body of bishops."[7]

The universality of the Church of Christ is equivalent to its catholicity, as the catechism of the German Bishops' Conference teaches. "Applied to the Church, [Catholic] means that the whole, worldwide, universal Church will announce the whole, true and genuine faith. The true Church is Catholic in distinction from communities that select only a part of the truth or wish to be a Church for only a particular people, a particular culture, a particular level, and so on."[8]

Moreover, the four marks of the Church are inseparable from one another. If one is lacking or diminished, the other three are also substantially affected. Fr. Yves Congar, O.P., has written: "Rather like the functions of Christ himself, the marks of the Church exist one within the other. . . . The unity of the Church is apostolic, holy and Catholic, its Catholicity is holy, one and apostolic, its apostolicity is Catholic, one and holy, and its holiness is apostolic, Catholic and one."[9]

If the Catholic Church is simply one of a number of particular Churches with "various degrees of density or fullness" (Sullivan), one can no longer perceive the Catholic Church as the unique "sacrament or instrumental sign of intimate union with God and of the unity of all humanity" (LG 1). The negative impact of such a perception on the Church's mission *Ad gentes* is devastating. Such an aberrant and novel view of the Catholic Church cannot but have a profoundly negative impact upon her missionary activity. In a clear reference to the evangelizing task of the Catholic Church, Vatican II teaches: "Missionary activity extends the saving faith of the Church. It expands and perfects its Catholic unity, it is sustained by its apostolicity, it activates the collegiate sense of its hierarchy and bears witness to its sanctity which it both extends and promotes" (*Ad gentes* 6).

The key to Sullivan's view is his theology of the *subsistit in* ("subsists in") of *Lumen gentium* 8. The correct interpretation of this *subsistit* is crucial for the future vitality of the Church's missionary activity.

---

7. Anton Angel, S.J., "Postconciliar Ecclesiology: Expectations, Results, and Prospectives for the Future," in *Vatican II: Assessment and Perspectives*, René Latourelle, ed. (New York: Paulist Press, 1988) 1:424–25.

8. The Church's Confession of Faith: *A Catholic Catechism for Adults*, Communion Books (San Francisco: Ignatius Press, 1987) 236.

9. Yves Congar, O.P., *I Believe in the Holy Spirit* (New York: The Seabury Press, 1983) 2:27.

The Congregation for the Doctrine of the Faith (CDF) has given two authentic interpretations of this phrase, one in *Mysterium Ecclesiae* in 1973, and the other in *Notificatio* concerning Leonardo Boff's book, *Church, Charism and Power,* in 1985. In the latter, CDF states: "The council had chosen the word *subsistit*—subsists—exactly in order to make clear that one sole 'subsistence' of the true Church exists, whereas outside her visible structure (*compagine visibile*) only elements of the Church (*elementa ecclesiae*) exist; these—*being elements* of the same Church—tend and conduct toward the Catholic Church."[10] This teaching of CDF should receive a wide and positive reception.

Father Sullivan contests the position of the Congregation, writing, "I do not see how one can justify such a claim." His position is in flat contradiction with the council and its *Acta*.

I note, first, that part of the problem is to be found in his inattentiveness to the Latin or Italian of the magisterium's documents. He consistently mistranslates the terms *compago socialis* and *compago* of *Lumen gentium* 8 and the CDF's declarations of 1973 and 1985 by the phrases "outside of the Catholic Church" or "outside of her limits." Yet neither *Lumen gentium* nor the CDF speaks of "limits" to the Church, which imply definite and clear boundaries; rather, *Lumen gentium* speaks of her communal and visible structure. Sullivan consistently ignores the subtleties of *Lumen gentium* 8 and of the Congregation, both of which reiterate that the Spirit of Christ acts *in and through* the social structure (*compago*) of the Church; both the divine and human elements of the Church are necessary. "The social structure of the Church serves the Spirit of Christ who vivifies the Church towards the growth of the body (see Eph. 4, 16)" (LG 8). It is "outside its [i.e., the Catholic Church's] structure [*compaginem*]," *Lumen gentium* continues (not outside its limits, as Sullivan translates), "[that] many elements of sanctification and truth are to be found which, as proper gifts to the Church of Christ, impel towards Catholic unity" (LG 8). With his insistence upon the impossibility of the "*absolute* and *exclusive* identity between the Church of Christ and the Catholic Church," (emphasis added) Sullivan falls into the reductionism of mathematical symbols that Cardinal Ratzinger warns against.

Second, Sullivan, noting that the council chose not to say that the Catholic Church is (*est*) the Church of Christ, has concluded therefrom that "the one fact that is absolutely certain is that the decision [of the council] no longer to say 'is' is a decision no longer to assert such

---

10. *Notificatio* of the Sacred Congregation for the Doctrine of the Faith, *Origins* 14 (April 4, 1985) 685.

absolute and exclusive identity between the Church of Christ and the Catholic Church."[11] Sullivan is wrong in his conclusion, but his position is also very mischievous for the missionary activity of the Catholic Church.

What is the significance of the substitution of *subsistit in* for *est*? The *Acta* could not be clearer. As Msgr. James T. O'Connor has concluded after studying the *Acta*, "number eight of *Lumen Gentium*, according to official explanation, intends to teach that there is only one Church of Christ and that this Church is found concretely in the Catholic Church."[12] Because the official explanation contained in the *Acta* is unequivocal, it is important to quote it in full:

> From the great number of observations and objections which were brought forth by the bishops in respect to this paragraph (as it appeared in the working draft), it is evident that the intention and context of this section were not clear to all.
>
> Now, the intention is to show that the Church, whose deep and hidden nature is described and which is perpetually united with Christ and His work, is concretely found here on earth in the Catholic Church. This visible Church reveals a mystery—not without shadows until it is brought to full light, just as the Lord Himself through His "emptying out" came to glory. Thus there is to be avoided the impression that the description which the Council sets forth of the Church is merely idealistic and unreal. Therefore, a clearer subdivision is set forth, in which the following points are successively treated:
>
> a) The mystery of the Church is present in and manifested in a concrete society. The visible assembly and the spiritual element are *not two realities*, but one complex reality, embracing the divine and human, the means of salvation and the fruit of salvation. This is illustrated by an analogy with the Word Incarnate.
>
> b) The Church is one only [*unica*], and here on earth is present in the Catholic Church although outside of her there are found ecclesial elements.

This clear understanding of the expression *subsistit in* is confirmed by an analysis of the teaching of the council on the relationship between the Catholic Church and the "ecclesial elements" present outside her visible structure. After analyzing the third section of the Decree on Ecumenism and the *Acta*, Msgr. O'Connor concludes, "It

---

11. Sullivan, "Significance," 274.
12. James O'Connor, "Is the Catholic Church the Church of Christ?" *The Fellowship of Catholic Scholars' Newsletter* (December 1990) 7–13.

can be deduced that the ecclesial elements and the means of salvation which are present in the separated churches and communities are present there to the extent of their union with the Catholic Church."[13]

To show that this is no innovation in the Church's teaching, Msgr. O'Connor quotes St. Augustine in his tract *On Baptism*: "There is one Church which alone is called Catholic; and whenever it has anything of its own in these communions of different bodies which are separate from itself, it is most certainly in virtue of this which is its own in each of them that she, not they, has the power of generation."

Separated Churches and communities function as means of salvation because elements of the Catholic Church subsist in them. This means that they draw their efficacy from the fullness of grace and truth found in the Catholic Church.

Having established that the teaching of the Second Vatican Council is that the Church of Christ and the Catholic Church are not two realities but one, I now wish to elaborate on the relationship of the Catholic Church to the peoples of the world. How does the Church exercise her saving mission over time to the billions of human beings who have lived or are now living in the world? A partial answer can be found in the stress the Second Vatican Council placed upon people "being related to the Catholic Church" rather than upon "membership in the Church."

Two elements moved the Second Vatican Council to this understanding of how people belong to the Catholic Church. One was the interpretation of the principle extending back to Origen of Alexandria and St. Cyprian of Carthage, "Outside the Church there is no salvation" (LG 2, 3, 13, 16; AG 7). The other was a reassessment of the meaning of membership in and ordination toward the Church (LG 13–16). The first principle is an assertion of faith upon which the Church's missionary activity is based; the second is a doctrinal elaboration of how the complementary and no less certain affirmation of the possibility of salvation for the "pagans" is in agreement with it. My concern here is about the possibility of salvation for "non-believers" and non-Catholic Christians and not with its actual realization, that is, with the summons God extends to everyone and not with the human responses to it.

I will discuss four sections of the Dogmatic Constitution on the Church, paragraphs 13, 14, 15, and 16, and conclude with the teachings of the Church found in the Pastoral Constitution on the Church in the Modern World and *Redemptoris missio*.

13. Ibid., 10.

The last section of paragraph 13 serves as a summary of the council's elaboration on the harmony existing between God's will for the salvation of all peoples and the necessity of the Catholic Church for salvation. "To this catholic unity of the People of God, which prefigures and promotes universal peace, all are called, and they belong to it or are related to it in various ways [*ad eamque variis modis pertinent vel ordinatur*] whether they be Catholic faithful or others who believe in Christ or finally all people everywhere who by the grace of God are called to salvation."

Before elaborating upon the teaching of Vatican II on this specific subject, I wish to show "how the idea of community and universality . . . permeates and shapes all the individual elements of [the Catholic] faith's content" (Joseph Ratzinger). Undergirding such an elaboration is the Church as the *Catholica*—a universality "in depth" (Henri de Lubac), embracing the whole of human nature because the Church sings always the canticle of universal charity: "Peace, the bond of holy fellowship, a building of living stones" (St. Augustine). What the Second Vatican Council reasserts along with the most ancient Christian tradition is that humanity is one, organically one by its divine origin and destiny. The *Catholica* is called to reveal to all peoples everywhere that original and pristine unity lost by sin, to restore and complete it.

St. Augustine explains the theology of the *Catholica* by framing a favorite patristic teaching on the unity of the human race in its origins with a fascinating image. After establishing a connection between the four letters of Adam's name and the Greek names for the four points of the compass, he continues: "Adam himself is therefore spread over the whole face of the earth. Originally one, he has fallen, and breaking up as it were, he has filled the whole earth with the pieces" (*On Psalm 96*, 15). Origen expressed the same theological anthropology: "Where there is sin, there is multiplicity" (*Ubi peccata, ibi multitudo*).

From the earliest times the Church has always had the sense of being "the third race," in which there was neither Jew nor Greek. The Church was conscious of carrying the true likeness of the Logos within herself. The destructive divisiveness of the human race after the Fall is portrayed in the dramatic story of the construction of the first human cities immediately before Abraham's call (Gen 11). The city built by the descendants of Noah repeated the fault of humankind's sinful ancestors who lived before the flood. People established an earthly city in order to assert their mastery over all things on earth and to reach immortality. But humankind was once again severely reprimanded by God, this time through the punishment of dissension arising from the confusion of languages. Their joint efforts turned into fratricidal conflict. *Ubi peccata, ibi multitudo*! The apparent unity of the builders of the tower of Babel was shown to be an illusion and its strength was shown to be a mere shadow. The true unity of humankind can be found only in the City of God, that is, in the charity and truth of the one and unique people of God.

The unity of the body of Christ supposes a previous natural unity of the human race in creation, as is so well expressed in the prayer of the Roman Missal (St. Pius V) to be spoken by the priest while mixing water and wine: "O God, you have established human nature in wondrous dignity and have even more wondrously renewed it" (*Deus, qui humanae substantiae dignitatem mirabiliter condidisti, et mirabilius reformasti*). In the beginning God created humanity as a whole. St. Irenaeus teaches that "in the beginning of time God plants the vine of the human race; he loved this human race and purposed to pour out his spirit upon it and to give it the adoption of sons" (*Adversus Haereses*, passim). The teaching of the Fathers of the Church is clear: the human race is one in its origins.

Since the whole human race was lost by the Fall, the Son of God had to become human in order to effect as such the re-creation of humankind. Irenaeus speaks about the recapitulation by Christ of the original human being: "When he became incarnate and was made man, he recapitulated in himself the long history of man, summing up and giving us salvation in order that we might receive again in Christ Jesus what we had lost in Adam, that is, the image and likeness of God" (*Adversus Haereses*, 3, 18, 1). Thus the human race, broken up and dispersed by sin, is again gathered up into the one body of Christ.

Cardinal Henri de Lubac, S.J., offers a theological reflection upon the teaching of the Fathers and, in my judgment, harmonizes the two doctrines previously adverted to: the necessity of the Church for salvation and God's universal salvific will.

> The human race is one. By our fundamental nature and still more in virtue of our common destiny we are members of the same body. Now the life of the members comes from the life of the same body. How, then, can there be salvation for the members if, on the impossible hypothesis, the body itself were not saved? But the salvation for this body, for humanity, consists in receiving the form of Christ, and that is possible only through the Catholic Church. For is she not the only complete, authoritative interpreter of Christian revelation? Is it not through her that the practice of the evangelical virtues is spread throughout the world? And, lastly, is she not responsible for the spiritual unity of men insofar as they will bind themselves to it? Thus this Church, which as

the invisible Body of Christ is identified with final salvation, as a visible and historical institution is the providential means of this salvation. As St. Augustine says, "In her alone mankind is refashioned and recreated."[14]

If I understand de Lubac correctly, he is saying that for humanity as a whole, that is collectively, there can be no salvation outside the Church. The Catholic Church is called to realize her absolutely necessary mission: to transform and complete human endeavor. The goal of the Church is eschatological salvation which can only be realized in a future world. The Second Vatican Council teaches that "the Church prays and works at the same time so that the fullness of the whole world may move into the People of God, the Body of the Lord and the Temple of the Holy Spirit, and that all honor and glory be rendered in Christ, the head of all, to the creator and Father of all" (*Lumen gentium* 17).

Recently, Pope John Paul II elaborated on the same doctrinal themes in his commentary on a text from St. Paul's Letter to the Ephesians. God "has made known to us the mystery of his will in accord with his favor that he set forth in him [Christ] as a plan for the fullness of time, to sum up all things in Christ, in heaven and on earth" (1:9-10). The Pope teaches: "The . . . Pauline texts regard the destiny of the human person, chosen and called to be an adopted child of God, not only in the individual dimension of the human race, but in its community dimension as well. God conceives, creates, and calls to himself a community of persons."[15]

With this insight that all created reality is to be seen in the light of divine revelation, we are now equipped to penetrate the teaching of the council. I wish to take up how Vatican II envisages the way in which all peoples either belong to or are ordained toward catholic unity. As I mentioned earlier, it is important to note that the final text of *Lumen gentium* chooses not to use the expression "members of the Church" which had been used by Pope Pius XII in his 1943 encyclical *Mystici corporis* and the preliminary conciliar text of 1962. Instead it speaks of the following:

(1) Catholics are those who "are fully incorporated into the society of the Church" (*plene incorporantur,* LG 14).

---

14. Henri Cardinal de Lubac, S.J., *Catholicism* (San Francisco: Ignatius Press, 1991) 223.

15. Pope John Paul II, General Audience Address, *L'Osservatore Romano,* English Edition, 31, 1202 (August 5, 1991) 7.

(2) Catechumens are those "who, under the impulse of the Holy Spirit, expressly ask to be incorporated into the Church [and] are by this very desire joined to it" (*hoc ipso voto cum ea coniunguntur,* LG 14). Thus, the traditional teaching on the "desire of the sacrament" (*votum sacramenti*) and "the desire of the Church" (*votum ecclesiae*), which formed in the past so prominent a part of the harmonization between the two doctrines of God's universal saving will and the necessity of the Church for salvation, is limited to the catechumens in the council text.

(3) Non-Catholic Christians: "The Church recognizes that it is joined to those who, though baptized and so honored by the Christian name, do not profess the faith in its entirety" (*coniunctam,* LG 15).

(4) Non-Christians: "Those who have not yet accepted the Gospel are related to the people of God in various ways" (*ordinantur,* LG 16).

Concerning the salvation of non-believers, *Gaudium et spes* 22 represents an advance over the discussion of *Lumen gentium*. The emphatic statement that the paschal mystery is the center of personal existence and human history makes it clear that the real agent of salvation can only be God, not ourselves; by its very nature the paschal mystery can only be received. The unsatisfactory expressions of *Lumen gentium* 16, in which human beings appear to be agents of their own salvation as seen in the verbs *quaerere* (seek), *adimplere* (fulfill), *conari* (strive), *possunt* (are able), *niti* (strive), are replaced by a phrase with the significantly passive verb, *consocientur* (being made partners): "We must hold that the Holy Spirit offers to all the possibility of being made partners, in a way known to God, in the paschal mystery" (*tenere debemus Spiritum Sanctum cunctis possibilitatem offerre, ut, modo Deo cognito, huic paschali mysterio consocientur, Gaudium et spes* 22).

One of the best statements of the universal possibility of salvation did not survive beyond text 4 (the Arricia text) of Schema 13, which was the original form of *Gaudium et spes*: "Because, however, Christ died for all men, we may also believe that the Spirit in a way known to himself gives all the possibility of conforming themselves to this [paschal] mystery."

Redemptoris missio inserts this teaching into the mainstream of the magisterium with a strongly pneumatological missiology. It appears to be a happy elaboration of *Gaudium et spes* 11, "impelled by its belief that it is being led by the Spirit of the Lord who fills the whole earth." Relying also upon the teaching of his earlier encyclical on the Holy Spirit, *Dominum et vivificantem* (DV), Pope John Paul II addresses the issue of the mission of the Church *ad gentes* (to the nations), that is, to the unbaptized: "The Spirit manifests himself in a special way in the

Church and in her members. Nevertheless, his presence and activity are universal, limited neither by space nor time" (28).

Later in a significant passage the Pope brings in two scriptural quotes contained originally in the Ariccia text of Schema 13, but omitted in the final text (see *Gaudium et spes* 11). "Thus the Spirit who 'blows whence he wills' (cf. Jn. 3:8, who 'was already at work in the world before Christ was glorified' and who 'has filled the world, . . . and holds all things together (and) knows what is said' (Wis. 1:7), leads us to broaden our vision in order to ponder his activity in every time and place" (RM 29). The next section is stated emphatically by the Pope.

> I have repeatedly called this fact to mind and it has guided me in my meetings with a variety of peoples. . . . Moreover, the universal activity of the Spirit is not to be separated from his particular activity within the Body of Christ, which is the Church. Indeed, it is always the Spirit who is at work, both when he gives life to the Church and impels her to proclaim Christ, and when he implants and develops his gifts in all individuals and peoples, guiding the Church to discover these gifts, to foster them and to receive them through dialogue (RM 29).

The significance of these additional and new texts in *Redemptoris missio* is major for several reasons.

First, the encyclical gives a stronger theological emphasis to the role of the Holy Spirit who is the climax of Jesus' messianic mission and who "becomes present in the Paschal Mystery in all of his divine subjectivity: as the one who is now to continue the salvific work rooted in the sacrifice of the Cross" (RM 21; see DV 42).

Second, the Church's magisterium of the 1990s no longer has difficulty in moving beyond the exigencies of historical exegesis; the Pope has made a strongly contemporary application of scriptural texts (see RM 29). Because texts from the Old Testament cannot be understood to contain the New Testament "as an integrating part of its own discrete or autonomous intelligibility,"[16] the Pope's use of a sense of scripture other than the literal emphasizes dramatically the free historical event of the Holy Spirit "who sows the 'seeds of the Word' in various customs and cultures, preparing them for full maturity in Christ" (RM 28).

Third, in the first three chapters of the encyclical, there is elabo-

---

16. Donald Keefe, S.J., "A Theological Metaphysics of History," unpublished text, 18.

rated a Trinitarian and doxological foundation for the Church's mission: the Church is gathered by and for the worship of the Lord of history, the Son who is sent by the Father to give the Spirit of adoption, the Spirit of the freedom of the children of the one Father, free in their Father's house.

Fourth, the salvation of the nations is clearly not a human work; the Holy Spirit is preeminently the principal agent of mission (RM III).

Behind this ecclesiology of the many modes of belonging to or being related to the Church is the basic teaching of the council concerning the Church as "the instrumental sign of intimate union with God and of the unity of all humanity" (LG 1). In each of the above-cited sections of *Lumen gentium*, especially 16, emphasis has been placed upon the following themes: the God of salvation, the unity of the human race in its origin and destiny, and the real oneness of Christ with this human race by virtue of the incarnation.

In concluding this section, I wish to emphasize that *Lumen gentium* speaks compellingly of the motive for mission in the Church. The council begins by referring to the widespread despair in modern society without Christ and concludes this section with a ringing call for mission. "More often, however, deceived by the evil one, people have gone astray in their thinking and exchanged the truth about God for a lie and served the creature rather than the creator (see Rom 1:21, 25), or living and dying in this world without God they are exposed to the extreme of despair. For this reason, to promote the glory of God and the salvation of all these people, the Church is mindful of the Lord's command: 'Preach the Gospel to the whole creation' (Mk 16:16), and so it assiduously encourages the missions" (LG 16).

2) The Saving Mission of the Catholic Church in the United States

Pope John Paul II emphasizes that it is "the witness of personal conduct" or "the witness of a Christian life which is the first and irreplacable form of mission" (RM 42). But as he observes, the missionary in the modern world is not necessarily sent to witness *ad gentes*. For most of our people, the missionary mandate of Jesus to his Church is experienced and lived in the apostolate of reevangelization here in the United States. In *Redemptoris missio*, the Pope states that "entire groups of the baptized have lost a living sense of the faith or even no longer consider themselves members of the Church and live a life far removed from Christ and his Gospel" (33).

The crisis of faith in the Catholic people is evidenced by the precipitous decline in many of the vital, that is, sacramental and catechetical, signs of the Catholic Church in the United States. Their decline in the Archdiocese of Denver is typical of Catholicism in the U.S.A. In 1967, two years after the Second Vatican Council, Sunday church attendance stood at seventy-seven per cent; today an optimistic count places it at thirty-eight per cent. Annual confirmations have fallen from nine thousand in 1966 to thirty-five hundred in 1989. Fifty-two per cent of our children between the ages of six and eighteen are not receiving any formal religious education. Only fifteen per cent of our children are in Catholic elementary and secondary schools compared to thirty per cent over a generation ago. Church marriages are also falling off but not precipitously.

The national Catholic vital statistics over the past generation indicate a similar decline in all areas with the exception of deaths, which have increased by eighteen per cent, and the general Catholic population, which has increased by twenty-seven per cent (see Appendix I). The statement made by the Fathers of the Second Vatican Council concerning the condition of today's humanity was prophetic. Especially remarkable in this respect is the seventh paragraph of *Gaudium et spes*: "The new conditions also affect the living of religion. . . . More groups of people are giving up the practice of religion. In contrast to earlier generations, it is not now unusual or just an individual matter to deny God or religion or to abandon them."

The challenge of a new evangelization of Catholics in the United States is staggering. Archbishop Edward McCarthy of Miami has said that the Catholic people constitute the largest religious group in our country, and fallen away and inactive Catholics constitute the next largest group.

A new evangelization of American society requires a radical "process of inculturation" (RM 52). It will be "a slow journey" (RM 52) because it is a renewal from within (EN 20). There is an instructive parallel for the late twentieth century to be found in the work of evangelization in sixteenth-century Europe by the two companions of St. Ignatius of Loyola, Claude LeJay and Alfonso Salmeron. Theirs was the long, tedious process of preaching and of directing the Spiritual Exercises for thousands in Europe. Only after decades was there a perceptible spiritual shift.

A new evangelization of culture is a glacial inching forward here and there. Change can be generated especially through the everyday level of person-to-person conversation, witness, and exchange. The Catholic Church in the United States is not called to flee the American culture, but rather to recognize that the determining characteristic of

Appendix I

General Summary Totals
Catholic Vital Statistics
(As per Official Catholic Directory)

	1966	1991	Increase (Decrease)
Priests	59,193	53,086	(11%)
Sisters	181,421	101,911	(44%)
High Schools Diocesan & Parochial Students	687,961	380,466	(45%)
High Schools Private Students	402,440	259,617	(36%)
Elementary Schools Diocesan/Parochial Students	4,409,476	1,929,184	(57%)
Elementary Schools Private Students	82,477	59,313	(28%)
Non-Residential Schools for Handicapped Students	12,051	9,767	(19%)
CCD High School Students	1,369,751	770,257	(44%)
CCD Elementary School Students	3,486,902	3,252,779	(7%)
Total Students under Catholic Instruction	10,911,213	6,661,383	(39%)
Infant Baptisms*	1,274,938		
Receptions into the Church*	123,149		
Total Baptisms & Receptions	1,398,087	1,147,976	(18%)
Marriages	355,182	336,645	(6%)
Deaths	389,938	457,337	+18%
Catholic Population	46,246,175	58,568,015	+27%

* 1991 combines infant baptisms and converts into one total for receptions into the Church.

modernity is the unparalled and radical break in the covenant between word and world. Ours is the time of the epilogue, of the afterword.[17] It is the period of the eclipse of the sign, and consequently a non-theological, even an anti-theological period. As Derrida says, only "the age of the sign is essentially theological."

A California pollster, George Barna, in a new book entitled *What Americans Believe*, states that the 1990s will be "the make-it-or-break-it era" for American Christianity. He is pessimistic about its outcome. His studies show that there will be a "religious revival, but not a Christian revival" in this decade. "More than before we are witnessing the entrenchment of what some refer to as 'secular humanist' attitudes. More individuals now believe that people are responsible only to themselves and that they determine their own destiny on the basis of their decisions and capabilities. I'm very worried about the Christian Churches. . . . The mainline denominations have been shrinking for years, but even now the evangelical churches are slowing down or reaching a plateau."

3) The Spirituality of Vatican II: *Lumen Christi* and Its Pastoral Implications

We fast approach the two-thousandth anniversary of the incarnation of the eternal Son of God. We must be realistic in admitting what we see everywhere before us: a great erosion of belief in the uniqueness of Christ and of the Christian faith from the American landscape. The next few years are given to the Church as a new advent. Pope John Paul II has described these years as "a new advent of grace opening up to the third millenium." As Mary, the Mother of God, pondered the archangel's words in her heart, that is, as she pondered the revelation of the mystery of the incarnation, the Church too is invited to ponder the Word of God in her heart, seeking to penetrate the unsearchable riches of Christ as they are revealed in creation, in the incarnation, in the redemption, and in the *nexus* between them.

Some pastoral conclusions can be drawn from our reflections on the theology of mission and its challenge in American culture.

I suggest that the Church throughout the United States reappropriate the leitmotiv of the Second Vatican Council, which is the paschal hymn (*Canticum Paschale*) sung to Christ by the Church in the

---

17. George Steiner, *Real Presences* (Chicago: University of Chicago Press, 1989).

darkness of the Easter Vigil before the Easter candle: *Lumen Christi*, Light of Christ. Its overriding preoccupation must be to say "yes"— *Lumen Christi, Lumen Ecclesiae, Lumen Gentium* (Light of Christ, Light of the Church, Light of Nations)—"yes" for the salvation, for the joy, and for the splendor of all humanity.

With an increasingly deepened interiority (GS 14), the Church must shine forth in the Taboric Light of Christ by living the paschal mystery throughout the liturgical year. Central to this encounter with the glorious countenance of the Risen Christ is the renewal of the sacrament of reconciliation. It is pastorally significant that the immensely popular Twelve-Step Program in its myriad manifestations has incorporated material elements of the Catholic sacrament of reconciliation. Any renewal of the Catholic Church must begin with a rediscovery of reconciliation and penance in the life and mission of the Church.[18]

We must renew Sunday Eucharist as "a special paschal feast" (*convivium paschale*, SC 47). The paschal Triduum must become in fact what it is in principle, the center of the liturgical year with its renewal each Sunday. Our goals must be specific. By the year 2000, the decline in Sunday Mass attendance must be reversed, and the Church everywhere must pray for and work for an average attendance of at least sixty-five per cent at Sunday Mass.

The renewal of catechesis must be founded on the four ancient rules or canons of faith (see Gal 6:16; 2 Cor 10:13-16; 1 Col 7:2; Irenaeus 1.9.4f.; Eusebius, *Hist. Eccl.* 6.13.5; Clement of Alexandria, *Stromata*, 7.15.90.2; Council of Laodicea in Phrygia, Council of Constantinople): the canon of sacred Scripture, the canon of baptismal creeds, the canon of Eucharistic prayers, and canon law. In each instance, the term "canon" should be understood as something sacred and therefore substantially normative. We must continually affirm

---

18. Such a renewal should be based on an understanding of history as a tridimensional plan which is concretely realized in the following orders:

"a) in the order of the divine economy (Old Covenant, New Covenant, Kingdom);

"b) in the order of history's sacramental representation (*sacramentum tantum, res et sacramentum, res tantum*);

"c) in the order of its scriptural tradition (the literal, the allegorical, and anagogical senses);

"d) in the order of its moral unity (our solidarity in the *sarx* of the first Adam, in the *mia sarx* of the New Covenant instituted by the second Adam, and in the *pneuma* of his resurrection);

"e) and in the order of liturgy (the Offertory, the Canon, the Communion)," Keefe, "History," 8.

with all pastoral clarity that in blessed Peter Jesus Christ "instituted a perpetual and visible principle and foundation for the unity of faith and communion" (LG 18). In relation to this renewal of catechesis, we should pray and work for a doubling of the number of students in grades one to eight under formal religious instruction in the United States and quadruple the number in grades nine to twelve. Even larger goals should be envisioned for those in adult religious education programs and campus ministry programs.

Special outreach must be made to Hispanic families and individuals. By the beginning of the third millenium, the Catholic Church in the United States should aim for at least three times the number of Hispanic surnamed persons enrolled in parishes than is now the case.

By the year 2000, the number of those confirmed should approximate the number of baptized according to the appropriate age and year.

The tripling of the number of seminarians in theology must be the subject of special prayer and activity during this new advent of grace which will bring us to the third millenium.

The Christian family should increasingly become the focus of the mission of the parish and the diocesan Church. The covenantal and nuptial significance of the human body should be presented along the lines of the theological anthropology of Pope John Paul II as developed in *Familiaris consortio*. We must pray and strive to reverse the drop in Church marriages by the year 2000.

In addition, more adequate pastoral care and service needs to be planned for and extended to the migrants and to the elderly in each local Church.

The cost of such an evangelization can be met through a comprehensive stewardship program organized throughout the United States.

To provide a focus for this process of renewal in the Archdiocese of Denver, we have commissioned a special icon of Our Lady of the New Advent. In the icon, Mary carries within her womb Jesus Christ our Savior, visible and teaching. His hand is raised in the traditional gesture of reconciliation and grace between God and all humanity.

The Church's virginal and maternal role towards humanity is patterned after that of the Blessed Virgin Mary. By keeping the faith integral and pure, in her preaching and ministry of baptism, the Church is called to bring "forth to new and immortal life children conceived of the Holy Spirit and born of God" (LG 64).

Each parish in the archdiocese will have the icon that has been commissioned of Mary, the Mother of Christ and of the Church. I am urging the whole archdiocese to pray in this new advent of grace for the opening of our Church to the graces of the new millenium.

Response

Joseph Augustine DiNoia, O.P.

I will forego the habitual temptation of respondents to present a new paper and try instead to restate and reinforce what I take to be the central argument of the theological portion of Archbishop Stafford's fine paper.

As I understand it, Archbishop Stafford's paper addresses an issue that has preoccupied—not to say mesmerized—Christian theologians and the Church itself since the Enlightenment: how can universally valid truths be embodied in a particular, historical revelation? In its common forms, this issue can be restated in terms of two subquestions: (1) how can a particular historical individual, Jesus of Nazareth, have been the agent of a salvation that is universal in scope? and (2) how can a particular historical community be the bearer of a universally applicable salvation? It is the second of these questions that receives most direct attention in Archbishop Stafford's paper, but the first, that is, the more Christological issue, is implicit as well.

Prevailing concerns about these questions are apparent in the way that different positions in the theology of religions and in missiology are classified. Recently, it has become common to contrast theological positions that are theocentric (universalistic) with those that are Christocentric or ecclesiocentric (particularistic) in emphasis. This classification is often deployed in modern theology in ways that suggest that particularistically framed positions must of necessity fail to affirm the universality of salvation. Archbishop Stafford's argument constitutes a direct challenge to this standard theological resolution of the issue of the scandal of the particular.

This resolution has been standard since the Enlightenment and has been developed by theologians since the nineteenth century under the influence of idealist philosophy. Basic to this resolution—as it has come to be shaped within the ambience of a broadly idealist theological and philosophical framework—is the notion that that which is universal always exceeds, transcends, or surpasses whatever is particular in manifestation. The particular limits and constrains the universal. At the most, the particular, the embodied, can be nothing more than the possibly dispensable occasion for access to the universal. By implication, the universally true and valid can be accessed independently of any of its particular embodiments or manifestations. This viewpoint is related to another that has become typical of modernity. It is the Cartesian suggestion that the true reality or identity of the person or the community is found not in its embodied form, but in its spiritual or disembodied form. The true self for the idealist resides in consciousness, not in the animated body that occupies space in the world. The true identity of a social entity is radically invisible. Bodiliness and structure are accidental rather than essential components of personal and social identity.

The impact of these ideas has been pervasive in all areas of Western theology, but particularly in the way that the universal scope of the Christian message is understood. There has been a strong temptation to affirm the universality of the salvation to which Christianity bears witness at the expense of the highly particularistic medium in which it is embedded. The intractably particularistic convictions of the Catholic mainstream seem, on this view, like a liability to be offset by emphasis on the universal, commonly accessible truths it enshrines but cannot be thought to monopolize. The particularism of the Christian idiom comes to be regarded as an embarassment, or at least as an obstacle to proclaiming its universally valid message.

Lately, powerful theological voices have been raised that challenge this standard view of the relation of the universal and the particular in Christian faith and proclamation. One thinks immediately, in this context, of Hans Urs von Balthasar, Henri de Lubac, and John Paul II, to mention only the leaders. Their significance lies in their unwillingness to accept the standard way of framing these issues and their determination to overcome the strictures imposed by the typical modern resolution of these issues. Archbishop Stafford's paper exemplifies an important strategy of this newly emerging theological movement: far from being embarrassing obstructions, Christian particularities constitute the indispensable mode of access to the universally valid truths of salvation.

In order to exhibit this strategy at work in Archbishop Stafford's paper, allow me briefly to restate the argument of its theological first section. There he argues two theses.

The first thesis is that the Catholic Church and the Church of Christ are one reality. Here is an important element in this new strategy for dealing with the relationship of the universal to the particular. Archbishop Stafford states: "Just as the Son of God assumed only one individual body for the ransom of humanity, so the Spirit of Christ through 'the social structure' of the Catholic Church (*socialis compago*) is the organ of salvation for the world." It is clear here that the particular is actively embraced: it constitutes the way in which we reach the universal. There is no suggestion, as in standard modern theology, that the particular poses obstacles to attaining the universal. The very particularity of Christ and the Church is the divinely constituted privileged mode of access to the universal, both for members of the community and for the world at large. In this conviction lies the significance of Archbishop Stafford's arguments for the coinherence of the marks of the Church and for his understanding of the *subsistit in*. These arguments are fundamental to his insistence that the visible assembly and the spiritual element are not separable, but one complex reality. The spiritual element in the Church's social reality is not something separable from its visible structure. This does not exclude, as Archbishop Stafford points out, the possibility that elements of the Catholic Church will exist elsewhere. There is no triumphalism here but a realistic acceptance of the structure of the divine plan as it has been revealed to us.

His second thesis is related to the first: the formula *extra ecclesiam nulla salus* (no salvation outside the Church) should be understood as affirming that there is no salvation outside of the Church for *humanity as a whole*. This is a point of capital importance. In effect, he proposes an eschatological reading of the notorious formula. The salvation of the world and of the human race within it depends in a way that is fundamentally mysterious on the fidelity of the Christian community to its Lord. It is only by being faithful to the details of the particularities of the paschal mystery that the Christian community will contribute to the realization of the salvation of the whole world. The greater our emphasis on the uniqueness, specificity, and particularity of the Christian faith, the more we will have served the divinely willed purpose of the salvation of the whole human race. Paradoxically, embrace of the particularity and specificity of the Christian faith entails not separatism and sectarianism, but true universalism. For it is only through reiteration of the promises contained in the specifically Christian story and through the memorial reenactment of salvation that the universal scope of this salvation becomes known and effective. The more we mute the specificity of the Christian ethos and idiom, the less we will contribute to the attainment of universal salvation. Rather than universalize and homogenize the Christian particular, the approach that is being offered here celebrates and accentuates the particular. It is only because of the salvation wrought in the particular, historical individual, Jesus Christ, that there is any universal salvation to be, with confidence, anticipated.

This is the key part of Archbishop Stafford's argument, as I understand it. I hope that he will recognize his argument in my restatement of it.

His argument points to the fundamental intelligibility of the divine plan in its dependence on the particular. We take it that the goal of the divine plan is the establishment of a "community of persons" (as Archbishop Stafford states, quoting Pope John Paul II), a communion with the triune God and with others in him. We are invited into the community of persons that is in the first place a trinity of divine persons. The community of created persons is welcomed into the community of the uncreated. This is God's purpose. If God's purpose is to be personally engaged with us, will he not come to us in the way in which personal engagements arise? That is to say, is it odd for God to have chosen to become personally engaged with us in the only way in which persons can identify and be engaged with other persons, namely in a bodily way? Is this as strange as modern theology would have us believe? We do not relate to the human race in general. We are suspicious of those who proclaim their devotion to humanity without ever seeming to commit themselves to any particular human beings. If, as we believe, God wants to be related to us, he must presumably make himself available as a person, as a person who is embodied and enfleshed, recognizable, with ancestors, with a mother and father, with relatives, with a language, with a country, with a culture, and so on. If God wants to become accessible to us in a personal way, he will become accessible as a particular person, not as a divinity in general, but as a person whom we can encounter, touch, hear, and speak to. Now I have been supposing that we actually believe that God intends this community of persons to be our final destiny, to constitute what we mean by salvation. Not supposing this, I grant that my argument would fail. But granting this, it seems to make good sense that God would come to us through the particular and through us to others.

III
The Church and Cultures

Francis E. George, O.M.I.

The Church has been, throughout the centuries, a creator of culture. Directly, as patron of great artists and musicians and architects, the Church commissioned the monuments of higher culture in the West. Indirectly, through the liturgy and popular devotions, the Church contributed to the shaping of languages and customs. That the lifestyle of the Christian faithful might be looked at anthropologically, as a particular expression of the human, as a way of distinguishing a "people," was not much reflected upon before the creation, in the late nineteenth century, of the discipline of cultural anthropology.

The first Catholics to enter into dialogue with cultural anthropology were theologians who created the new discipline of missiology. Among them were a number of German Divine Word Missionaries and Oblates of Mary Immaculate. Although the founders of cultural anthropology, such as Edward Burnett Tylor, were basically hostile to any form of religious belief, missiologists soon began using the data, hypotheses, and conclusions of anthropologists in order to understand better the people to whom missionaries were sent and to learn how to communicate the gospel message more effectively across cultural barriers. More recently, missiologists have been in conversation with anthropologists such as Clifford Geertz, Victor Turner, and Mary Douglas in order to understand more adequately the dynamics of cultural change as well as to find help in explaining the cultural and therefore religious pluralism which has somehow to be joined with our belief in Christ's uniqueness.[1]

1. See Robert J. Schreiter, "Anthropology and Faith: Challenges to Missiology," *Missiology* 19 (1991) 283–94; John A. Saliba, "Religion and the Anthropologists,

The first official Church documents to engage culture in the anthropological sense were Vatican II's Constitution *Gaudium et spes* and the Conciliar Decree *Ad gentes*. It was a friendly engagement, begun in the context of the council's desire to institute a new dialogue between the Church and the world. In opening the Second Vatican Council, Pope John XXIII distinguished between the "substance of the ancient doctrine of the *depositum fidei*" and "the formulation of its presentation."[2] This distinction, in the light of linguistic theories current today, could be criticized as rationalistic. Cultural forms and linguistic expressions are not distinguished from the thoughts or message they carry as accidents are distinguished from substances in classical philosophy. A change of linguistic form inevitably entails some change in the understanding of content, at least by way of new connotations. A change of words influences the way we think. This truth has long been recognized by missionaries who have had to choose which of many possible translations might be most suitable for expressing the truths of faith in language different from that in which they themselves first heard the gospel. Nevertheless, Pope John's distinction forced a consideration by the council of the cultural trappings of the faith. Discussion of the relation between Church and world quickly became an increasingly rich conversation about the relation between faith and cultures.

When the council turned its attention to the Church's life *ad intra*, in *Lumen gentium*, it did not yet find it necessary to speak of culture. *Lumen gentium*, however, does speak of the relation of individual peo-

---

1960–1976," *Anthropologica* 18 (1976) 179–213 and 19 (1977) 177–208; and John Ball, "Anthropology as a Theological Tool: I. Culture and the Creation of Meaning," *Heythrop Journal* 28 (1987) 249–62, and "Anthropology as a Theological Tool: II. Symbol and the Efficacy of Ritual," *Heythrop Journal* 28 (1987) 405–17. The first American missiologist to make the findings of cultural anthropology practically available to missionaries was Louis Luzbetak, SVD. See *The Church and Cultures: New Perspectives in Missiological Anthropology* (Maryknoll, N.Y.: Orbis Press, 1988).

2. Discourse of Pope John XXIII for the opening of the Second Vatican Ecumenical Council, October 11, 1962, AAS 54 (1962) 792. Implicitly, Pope John's statement seems to support an instrumentalist view of language, regarding language as the means whereby a speaker gives expression to thoughts which exist independently of the language, through the employment of words whose meanings are the object of explicit agreement between prospective speakers. By contrast, an expressivist view of language holds that thought has no determinate content until it is expressed in a shared language. Speech as symbolic discourse can occupy the middle ground between these two theories.

ples to the one people of God.³ In the universal Church, the particular Churches share spiritual goods, each bringing its own gifts and thereby contributing to the fullness of Catholic unity. Ecclesial unity is possible across cultural diversity because faith brings to fulfillment whatever is positive in any culture. Faith, in *Lumen gentium*, is seen as completing culture, but little attention is paid in this document to how the faith itself might be affected by being expressed in new cultural forms. Nor does any culture, precisely as culture, "reveal" something of Christ.

When the council turned its attention to the Church's action *ad extra*, in *Gaudium et spes* and then in *Ad gentes*, the Fathers began to speak for the first time explicitly of culture. Whereas a concern for Catholic unity pervades *Lumen gentium*, a celebration of human pluralism characterizes *Gaudium et spes*. "The word 'culture' in a general sense," the Constitution teaches, "refers to all those things which go to the refining and developing of man's diverse mental and physical endowments . . . culture necessarily has historical and social overtones, and the word 'culture' often carries with it sociological and ethnological connotations; in this sense one can speak about a plurality of cultures."⁴ The council went on to teach that a culture is to be judged adequately human to the extent that it enables those who share it to grow in their "ability to wonder, to understand, to contemplate, to form personal judgements and to cultivate a religious, moral and social sense."⁵

Even as it began to formulate criteria for judging the evangelical adequacy of a particular culture, the council manifested particular interest in what it called "new culture" or "new humanism," a development marked by the universal mass phenomena which have become even more evident in the twenty-five years since the council. Much of Vatican II's perceived optimism about the human condition stems from its positive reading of the development of mass media of communication, of progress in economic life and the opening of political life to greater participation by all, of the creation of world-wide communities of scientists and the placing of technological advance at the service of all peoples. The diversity of languages and cultures celebrated in *Gaudium et spes* is immediately counter-balanced by a certain delight in global movements which, in some sense, are used as analogues of the universality of the Church herself and can be vehicles

3. *Lumen gentium*, 13 and 17.
4. *Gaudium et spes*, 53.
5. *Gaudium et spes*, 59.

for her message if only she can enter into dialogue with them. For behind the openness of Vatican II to worldly development stands the faith conviction that the Head of the Church is also Lord of the World. Faith and culture are never collapsed into each other, never identical; but neither should they be enemies. The relationship, the dialogue, should be friendly.

The council's document on the missions (*Ad gentes*) evaluates human cultures even more positively than does *Gaudium et spes*. Cultures are more than passive receptacles for reexpressing universal Christian faith; they have within them positive elements, authentic human values which have functioned secretly as *semina verbi*, preparing a people to hear the explicit proclamation of God's word when the moment comes to receive Christian missionaries. Missionary activity therefore imitates "the plan of the Incarnation."[6] Each time the gospel is proclaimed in another language, the word takes on flesh anew.

This quick glance at three documents of Vatican II shows how the seeds of what is now called "inculturation of the faith" and, from another perspective, "evangelization of culture" were planted in the soil of the council. They put down roots in the teaching of Paul VI and have flowered in a particularly exuberant way in the magisterium of John Paul II. Teaching on the relationship between faith and culture is continuously being expanded, even in the recent encyclicals, *Centesimus annus* and *Redemptoris missio*, and in the *lineamenta* for the upcoming European and African synods. Rather than trace this rich development in magisterial teaching now, I want instead to make use of it to clarify points central to relating Church and cultures and, finally, I will suggest a way of doing mission today which would reflect the Church's convictions about her relationship to cultures. First, I will set forth five points which, I believe, can justifiably be drawn from the ecclesial conversations about faith and culture since Vatican II, and second, I will draw a sketchy map to show how we might walk in mission while continuing to talk, continuing the conversation about the relationship between Church and cultures by allowing it to affect all other missionary activity.

Talking Points

1. An evangelized culture has theological weight. In some sense culture is a theological *locus*, and discussion of culture is, therefore, as important to the Church as discussion of grace or of nature. John Paul

---

6. *Ad gentes*, 22.

II said this very clearly in 1982 in a statement he has repeated *verbatim* in many other contexts: "A faith which does not become culture is a faith not fully received, not entirely thought through, not faithfully lived."[7] Also in 1982, when the Pope established the Pontifical Council for Culture, he stated: "The synthesis between culture and faith is a demand not only of culture but also of faith."[8]

On the one hand, this means that, as a particular people or cultural group enters into faith with more familiarity and profundity, the object of their belief, the revealed mystery which is the criterion for the truth of their faith, is itself probed more exhaustively through being examined in a new cultural context. A mystery of faith might come to be understood more deeply by the universal Church because of insights garnered from the dialogue between faith and culture in one part of the Church.

On the other hand, the self-consciousness born of dialogue with the demands of faith in believers' lives and with already evangelized cultures elsewhere is a new form of awareness within a culture, opening it, purifying it, transforming it. The transformed culture of a people baptized in Christ's name, accepting his gospel, and living in his Church is a place (*locus*) for all of us to look for deeper understanding of revelation, because an evangelized culture manifests Christ (it shows how Christ can be African, Chinese, American); it mediates God's grace (it is itself a kind of covenant reality which can serve as substratum for receiving the covenant of grace); and it contributes to the coming of God's reign (it brings to the final recapitulation of all things in Christ a particular way of being human).

2. Important though faith and culture are to one another, the Church has not attempted to impose on the dialogue a single definition of culture. John Paul II often refers to culture, broadly speaking, as the realm of the human as such. Perhaps more useful in many discussions is an understanding of culture as the sum total of one's non-biological inheritance. Fr. Avery Dulles has given us a description very useful for theological purposes: "By a culture we usually understand a system of meaning and values historically transmitted, embodied in symbols, and instilled into the members of a sociological group so that

---

7. John Paul II, Address to the Congress of the "Movimento Ecclesiale di Impegno Culturale," January 16, 1982, *La Traccia*, no. 1 (February 15, 1982) 55–57, 2. This quote reappears in many different talks and letters.

8. John Paul II, Address to the participants in the meeting of the Comitato di sostegno e di promozione del Centro Cattolico Internazionale per l'UNESCO (Cic), May 24, 1982, LT 3, no.5 (June 15, 1982) 694–96,3.

they are spontaneously inclined to feel, think, judge and behave in certain characteristic ways."[9] Culture is second nature.

It seems to me that, in the conversation between faith and culture, any definition of culture is helpful provided it does not reduce culture to an epiphenomenon of economic activity or biology or psychology. Because culture is not reducible to clearly observable phenomena available for mathematical analysis, which are the usual object of scientific study, many anthropologists, who want always to consider themselves scientists, have found in the human ability to make symbols of material things an activity which enables them to study economic, biological and psychological phenomena as cultural realities, without reductionism. Culture therefore designates "a class of things and events dependent upon symboling that are considered in a kind of extra-human context."[10] Symbols have their own lives.

Theological definition of the process of inculturation of the faith is, however, more explicit.[11] First, inculturation is not the relationship between an individual and his or her faith community. Accepting the faith as a child is similar to an infant's assuming a culture. This process used to be called "socialization" and is now more often called, among English-speaking anthropologists, "enculturation." As an individual, each believer is enculturated in the faith. Second, inculturation is not the term for the interaction between a missionary's culture, historically influenced by the faith, and the culture of a people to whom he or she goes to preach the gospel. Whenever two cultures meet, both change; and this process, this dialogue between the missionary's culture and that of the people whom he or she serves, is called "acculturation." Nor is inculturation, third, the name for an extrinsic relation between faith and culture, as if they were not intrinsically, even symbiotically, related. Missiologists, therefore, no longer use terms like "adaptation" or "adjustment"; and even terms like "localization" and "indigenization" are considered too narrow in meaning to express what happens when faith is inserted into a culture and finds a true home there. This is inculturation of the faith: it "means the intimate trans-

---

9. Avery Dulles, S.J., *The Catholicity of the Church* (Oxford, 1985) 175

10. Leslie A. White, "Human Culture," in *Encyclopedia Britannica*, 15th ed. (Chicago: 1977) 8:1152–53; see also, Raymond Firth, *Symbols Public and Private* (London: Allen and Unwin, 1973), especially chap. 5, "Modern Anthropological Views of Symbolic Process," 165–206.

11. Jose Saraiva Martins, *Missione e Cultura* (Rome: Urbanianum 1986) 19–22. The term 'inculturation' was apparently used for the first time in 1962 by Father J. Masson, S.J.

formation of authentic cultural roles through their integration in Christianity and the insertion of Christianity in the various human cultures."[12]

The other side of inculturation of the faith is evangelization of culture. When believers search in their own culture for the resources necessary for expressing their faith, they may discover that the culture lacks terms and values needed to incarnate the gospel adequately. Cultures blind as well as guide, and believers will often have to invent new cultural symbols inspired by the faith itself. They will also inevitably find in their culture positive obstacles to understanding the faith and living the gospel, and these obstacles to faith will have to be transformed or eliminated from their culture. Awareness that every culture, while it is a substratum for faith, is in some way also demonic or sinful has led some believers to insist that the gospel and the community which proclaims it are inevitably counter-cultural.

3. The Church is herself both the context of the inculturation process and, in part, the object of the process. This is still a controverted point. Some theologians, mostly Protestant, insist that the only "universal" in Christian faith is Jesus Christ himself. Once he is proclaimed, how he is followed and what shape the community which gathers in his name will take are matters that can then be decided by a newly evangelized cultural group on its own. The important thing is to accept Christ. Most missiologists would hold, however, that both Christ and the entire gospel message are to be inculturated. There is one Christ and one gospel, which imposes a certain consistency in evangelical discipline everywhere. Not only is Christ proclaimed and accepted, but his teaching is also to be used as a universal guide. Catholic theologians, it seems to me, must also argue that the Church herself, as faith reality, is the object of inculturation. The universal Church herself and the ecclesial structures which are given *jure divino* must be incarnated in different cultures and thereby find new forms of expression.

The necessary links among the person of Christ, the gospel message, and the ecclesial community, among common Lord, common faith, and common baptism (Eph 4:5), explain also why the Church is the context for the inculturation process. Christ cannot be known for who he truly is outside the Church which is his body. And the gospel cannot be adequately understood outside of the community which gave it birth and which interprets it anew from age to age. There is no text without a context. Inculturation, therefore, cannot take place outside an explicitly ecclesial community. The inculturation dialogue be-

---

12. John Paul II, *Redemptoris missio*, 52.

comes aberrational when its points of reference are only "truths of faith" on the one hand and a culture basically foreign to the Church on the other. The Church, in mediating this dialogue between faith and culture, must be party to it, thereby developing deeper insights into her own nature and mission.

4. Both Paul VI and John Paul II often repeat two principles for judging the inculturation process: 1) the culture being taken up by and into the faith must be compatible with the gospel; and 2) communion with the universal Church must be maintained.[13] Together, these very general rules preserve the relation between Church and culture as the faith searches for new expression in a recently evangelized culture.

Since inculturation is basically a new name, in an anthropologically sophisticated age, for a process which began in New Testament times, Catholics might search in past theological discussions for rules to flesh out these two general principles. In fact, many of the traditional "rules for the development of doctrine" in the Catholic sense can serve missiologists and others who want to judge whether a new expression of revealed truth or a new formulation of Church teaching is compatible with the gospel. And more recently developed "guidelines for inter-faith dialogue" can assist those who want to be sure that a new inculturation strengthens rather than weakens communion with the universal Church. As the Church welcomes a diversity of cultural expressions of the Catholic faith, inter-cultural dialogue must become an intra-ecclesial exercise.

A moment's reflection shows why both these general principles and the rules which preserve their intent are necessary. The cultural and historical situation of the Jerusalem Church of the first Christian century cannot be replayed hundreds of years later. Later formulations of Church teaching and centuries of experience of Christian living cannot be skipped over in an attempt to get back to some hypothetical "pure gospel," as if the Holy Spirit's action in history had no importance for faith today or as if previously evangelized peoples had no role to play in informing the faith of those now accepting Christ for the first time. The dialogue necessary for inculturating the faith is therefore a dialogue in history and also with history: the history of the faith, the history of the Church, and the history of this people, newly coming to know Christ and his Church.

5. Who then is responsible for inculturating the faith locally and evangelizing the culture which is to serve as faith's vehicle for future generations of a recently converted people? The process of inculturat-

---

13. John Paul II, *Familiaris consortio*, 10.

tion is an integrated movement, a constant and lengthy interaction among three parties: 1) the evangelizer, who generally comes from a foreign culture; 2) the evangelized, with their own beliefs and way of life; and 3) the larger Church, with her own diverse cultural traditions. In this interaction, there is a first moment when someone witnesses, proclaims, serves. In the beginning, these activities are planned and explained by missionaries who are foreign to the culture. They bear responsibility for the truth of what they say and do and for constructing the first bridge over the gap between their message and the culture of their listeners, between the faith itself and the lives of those to be converted to Christ. There must then come a moment of discernment about this culture's capacity to receive the gospel, and at the same time there is an assimilation of the gospel to the culture. At this point, the new converts must be very actively involved, and some explicit conversation with the larger Church will be necessary, especially through dialogue with the pope and bishops who are, as successors to the apostolic college, finally responsible for overseeing both the handing on of the deposit of faith and the evangelizing of the world. Finally, steps must be taken to transform the culture in the light of the gospel; and responsibility for this must rest, it seems to me, primarily with those who are both of the faith and of the culture. Does what the Church teaches about family life, about war and peace, about the creation of the natural world and its integrity, about the nature and dignity of the redeemed human person find a home in this culture?[14] These questions shape a dialogue which every believer, in every culture and every age, must carry on within his or her own mind and heart. Proof of a successful inculturation is the production of a new synthesis, a new expression of the gospel, capable of guiding lives in an evangelized culture and recognizable to all in the universal Church as authentic, as a particular contribution to universal communion.

What happens when evangelization fails to inculturate the faith and therefore does not result in an evangelized culture? When the faith is not adequately inculturated, Christianity finds expression as a new form of docetism or angelism. An abstract Christianity, stripped of its own history and recreated along essentialist lines, must remain an unincarnated system. When, on the other hand, a culture is not adequately evangelized, it remains inappropriately normative for faith. The result is some form of religious syncretism.

The Old Testament is witness to the mixture of Yahwehistic monotheism with various pagan rites and practices. The prophets de-

---

14. John Paul II, *Centesimus annus*, 49–52.

nounced idolatry, and the scribes perfected the law to protect the purity of Jewish faith. The power of God's word gradually purified various cultural practices of the Hebrews, and the same power is the ultimate reason for confidence in the outcome of any authentic process of inculturation (1 Cor 1:17). Practically, the always present possibility of syncretism warns against ever bringing complete closure to the inculturation dialogue. A confused unity testifies to an inadequate evangelization of culture.

A related religious phenomenon, parallelism, also attests to an inadequate evangelization of culture. Parallelism occurs when the culture accepts and legitimates the practice of two distinct religious systems. Each remains itself and operates alongside the other. Examples can be found in the religious practices of some of the native peoples of both North and South America and, in more sophisticated form, among the Japanese. Parallelism highlights the problem of judging what conversion to the Christian faith really demands. Its possibility warns the evangelizer to check continuously on the real significance, in a given culture, of traditional Christian symbols.

Before concluding this section, let me introduce into the conversation two unsubstantiated hypotheses about failed or problematic relationships between authentic Christian faith and our own culture, American culture. The first is a conjecture about syncretism in American religious history, and the second is a more recent example of angelism or alienation.

I would like to submit that the two archetypically American syncretic religions are Unitarianism on the left and Mormonism on the right. Both reject fundamental revealed truth about the nature of the Godhead. Unitarianism isolates the Spirit by making the Spirit wholly immanent. In Emerson's words, we are all part of the Oversoul. Secularized in Dewey, this religious assertion reduces God to a name for the sum total of human ideals and values. American liberals coopt the Spirit. Mormonism, on the other hand, isolates the Word by taking it entirely literally and creating a new religious history separate from authentic revelation but exactly expressive of a certain collective American religious experience. American conservatives coopt the Word. In both cases, revelation is distorted to conform to American experience, either internal, psychological, or external, historical. The result is syncretism: revealed truths not inculturated but themselves changed to conform to cultural proclivities in a new syncretic religion.

A more recent clash between ethical demands rooted in a gospel vision and American resistance to them shows, I believe, how missionaries can unwittingly be caught up in angelism because of inadequate sensitivity to the culture of the people to whom they are proclaiming the gospel. The case in point is reverse mission, the attempt by American overseas missionaries to return to this country and help people here understand what the gospel asks of us vis à vis international solidarity for justice. Too often, it seems to me, this constitutive dimension of the gospel message has come cloaked in various interpretations of history which are not only extraneous to the gospel itself but also positively opposed to some basically salvageable values of American culture. Have American missionaries taken our own culture seriously, respecting the people here in the same way we attempt to respect the people to whom we were first sent in other countries? To force an American to choose between justice and liberty, for example, is an unacceptable demand in this culture. A message which dismisses the entire history and experience of this country as just another example of "bourgeois liberalism" deserves itself to be dismissed. Such a "gospel" can never be inculturated; it will remain a case of abstract Christianity, of angelism.

Unfortunately, a message so easily ignored makes it all the more difficult to address the foundational religious reason for calling the United States to change in the light of gospel demands. This country has seen itself as the successor of ancient Israel, a uniquely chosen people, a people who, by reason of their citizenship, consider themselves the Church. In its secularized version, this claim is attached to democracy, of which the United States becomes the citadel and the touchstone, the measure for all other countries. Since there is no divine mandate for such a claim, it is idolatrous; but it is powerful and deserves to be addressed seriously by missionaries who want to inculturate Catholic faith in this society.

Walking While Continuing to Talk

If the full understanding of who Jesus is cannot be attained apart from the experience of ecclesial communion, then proclaiming the gospel means not only calling individuals to believe in him but also constructing an ecclesial context of belief. When proclaiming the gospel is understood as a process which includes inculturating the faith, evangelization becomes an activity introducing new believers to the experience of a Church which will be at home in their culture. The faith can be expressed in new cultural forms only from within an inculturated Church. Studies which discuss only the inculturation of the kerygma are not enough. The missionary, by careful attention to both the doctrine of the faith and the relationships which shape the Church everywhere, must at the same time both proclaim Christ and form an inculturated Church.

Introducing ecclesial experience means recreating locally the relations named by the images or symbols for Church in Scripture: body, bride, family, people. These are the relations which create and express ecclesial communion. Experiencing these relationships in a culturally distinctive way forms a self-conscious local Church able to inculturate the Catholic faith.

Symbols both communicate meanings and express communion. The symbol invites both thought and union, to paraphrase Paul Ricoeur. As evangelizers reinterpret symbols of faith in a new ecclesial context, they walk or move back and forth between translating meanings and creating ecclesial community. The process encompasses the following "steps":

1. During a period of study of the culture before explicit evangelization, the missionaries try to discover how the relations of ecclesial communion named by biblical images—the relation between mother and child, between bridegroom and bride, between the head and the members of a social body, the relation characterizing associations with a common spirit—are lived and experienced locally, in the people's culture. Taking this step probably requires at least some of the tools of semiotic analysis of cultural meanings and of phenomenological analysis of cultural consciousness.

2. After a first proclamation of the gospel, as a small group of people gradually form around their common acceptance of Christ as Savior, relationships begin to be created. The evangelizer fosters these relationships while instructing the catechumens in the faith of the universal Church. The group remains in the dominant culture; it resists becoming a sect.

3. The group's experience, founded on many individuals' decision to accept Christ as prophet, priest, and king and to live in him in relationship with other believers, begins to be expressed in terms familiar to this people's culture. They are already body, bride, family, people in their own culture and are beginning to understand how life as Church modifies these relationships. At the same time, the new Church actively reaches out to incorporate the experience of the entire Catholic Church. Believers are aware that they are modifying old relationships and introducing new relationships into their society, that their cultural horizon is being expanded. It is now in the whole Christ that they are body, bride, family, people. These relationships, while new in scope, are modeled to the extent possible on the pattern already in the culture; yet, in ecclesial communion, these relationships are also person-

alized in modalities which are new to the culture. Local believers, through common words and collective gestures, develop a communal self-consciousness which enables them to profess that they are the Church, both particular and universal. From within the experience of the network of ecclesial relationships, believers continue to search for ways of expressing the content of their faith in the symbols, myths, and gestures familiar to their culture.

4. The young Church comes to a point of maturity in which she has re-expressed in local symbols at least some of the relations that constitute her experience and is able to "do theology" out of her culturally distinctive experience of Christ, the gospel, and the Church. These new formulations of faith can enrich the universal Church's vocabulary and might offer the whole Church new forms of prayer, organization, and activity. The young Church at this point is sensitive to her local culture's unity, emphases, and agenda so as to bring the faith into active dialogue with the culture as it understands itself. Pastoral leaders in the particular Church will be gradually developing the hermeneutical skills necessary to interpret their people's life and beliefs for all in the universal Church.

5. Problems with living the faith fully in the local culture and misunderstandings which complicate dialogue and relationship with other particular Churches in the universal communion of faith show where the local culture must be transformed by faith. Obstacles to either inculturation or ecclesial communion, dissonance in the conversation, bring believers to awareness that their culture is deficient in some way. It must change by becoming more open to Christ and to the gospel. The Church, guided by her local pastors and in communion with the bishop of Rome, begins to decide on an agenda for deepening her faith and transforming the culture.

6. As the local Church joyfully experiences the fullest possible ecclesial communion, she is moved by consciousness of her own inner life to search for ways of including all members of the local culture in the experience of Church. The inculturated Church formulates a plan for inculturated evangelization. She wants to speak of her Lord and communicate his message and life to those who share her people's culture without yet sharing their belief. In this action, she becomes effectively an open sign, putting her own life into a process of questioning and dialogue.

While the last three steps in this process depend both logically and existentially on the first three, there is no strictly linear pattern or progress. The process is organic; any part demands the whole. An ecclesial program will emphasize now one point and then another, depending on particular circumstances. Both the foreign evangelizers and the native-born pastors and believers need a broad vision which synthesizes the faith, the Church, and the local culture. Without such a vision, the part risks being taken for the whole, mistakes will be made in mission, and evangelization will be less coherent.

Inculturating the faith by shaping the fundamental relations of ecclesial communion, as they are described in the New Testament, according to the pattern of how a local culture experiences these relations, brings a new consciousness of Church into universal ecclesial conversation. This conversation broadens the local culture's horizons because it extends its people's relationships to believers outside the culture. Foreigners become part of the culture's consciousness through their relationship to those in the culture connected to them through ecclesial communion.

The same process, however, also shows the universal Church how to incorporate diversity and difference in new ways. It can have consequences for extending ecclesial communion itself. The inculturated evangelization outlined above might furnish object lessons in how to broaden Catholic communion, how to discuss new ways of reaching that consensus in faith and action necessary for unity among all Christian Churches and ecclesial communities. Churches are cultural systems, tissues of culturally mediated relationships and networks of culturally conditioned actions. When relationships are extended and when actions unite across cultural boundaries, new ways of understanding develop. Inculturating the faith locally can increase sensitivity to possible new horizons for Christian unity.[15]

It can also open new horizons for human unity. There are as many histories as there are persons and peoples, but the theological significance of human history depends on a reading of the nature of human unity in the light of God's Word. When history is read as a "dialogue of liberty with God,"[16] the world becomes a stage on which some actors accept God's gift of the Spirit and speak new words, while others reject this gift and are trapped in a script of their own making.[17]

---

15. See Avery Dulles, "Paths to Doctrinal Agreement," *Theological Studies* 47 (1986) 32–47

16. John Paul II, Address to the Fifth Symposium of the Council of European Bishops' Conferences, October 5, 1982, AAS 74 (1982) 1255–60, 3.

17. See John Paul II, *Dominum et vivificantem*, 46–48. See also Hans Urs von Balthasar, *Man in History: A Theological Study* (London: Sheed and Ward, 1968) 178: "Nothing in the growth of secular history is a clear sign, unmistakable to a neutral intelligence, that we stand at a particular point of salvation history."

The Church's role in this history is to proclaim God's Word in all circumstances and to discern the movement of the Spirit in the world. The Church discerns the Spirit's action in the world through analysis of her own self-consciousness, once she has taken to herself the "joy and hope, the grief and anguish" of all peoples.[18] She reads these human emotions as moments of consolation and desolation in humanity's movement toward unity with God. She is able to read the signs of the times because the Spirit shows her how to distinguish *chronos*, the course of time, from *kairos*, the time of grace, and the contrast between these two rhythms of time fuels spiritual discernment. The movements of grace in an individual's experience of God in prayer, in the world's movement towards God's reign, and in the stages of the Church's own self-consciousness as she strives to follow her Lord are all objects of the Church's scrutiny. In weaving all these experiences together, she develops her sense of what it means to be a sacrament of unity and a sign of hope for all. In faith, she waits for complete unity in God's own time.

Because God's time is simultaneous, it makes sense to speak in human time, which is successive, of an *ecclesia ab Abel*, a Church born from Abel the just, existing from the beginning of human history.[19] The Church, in this broad sense, has always accompanied men and women as they have journeyed through history, because the Church expresses their relationships with the eternal God, their communion with him and with each other in him. In a pilgrim Church, men and women talk while they walk: "While they were talking and discussing together, Jesus himself drew near and went with them. . . . And he said to them, 'What is this conversation which you are holding with each other as you walk?' . . . They said to each other, 'Did not our hearts burn within us while he talked to us on the road, while he opened to us the scriptures?'" (Luke 24:15, 17, 32). The Church exists in conversation, in speech-acts which continuously proclaim and reinterpret the resurrection of her Lord, really present in the symbolic words and gestures of the Church, especially in Eucharistic sharing.[20]

---

18. *Gaudium et spes*, 1; see also John Paul II, *Dominum et vivificantem*, 26.

19. See Yves Congar, "Ecclesia ab Abel," *Abhanglungen über Theologie und Kirche*, eds. Heinrich Elfers and Fritz Hoffman (Dusseldorf, 1952) 79–108.

20. *To the Ends of the Earth*, the 1986 U.S. Bishops' pastoral statement on world mission, interprets mission in Eucharistic terms, making good use of John 6 along with the more classical missionary texts from the Synoptics and Paul's Epistle to the Romans. The pastoral statement thereby situates all missionary activities (see chapter 5 of John Paul II, *Redemptoris missio*) in the context of sharing divine truth and life, an emphasis in full accord with the ecclesiology of *Lumen gentium*.

The Church is a *sacra conversazione*. In paintings of this genre each saint, from his or her time, place, and culture, stands next to another. Each can be taken to represent a particular Church, a distinctive expression of the common faith. All are able to speak together, to speak from their differences, because all surround Jesus in the arms of his mother. They speak to him and through him. Mary presents him and listens. The picture potentially includes saints from all cultures. The conversation is truly sacred; it is a conversation in faith brought to fulfillment in beatific vision. When believers live the faith in a local Church at home in their culture, the conversation is also truly their own.

Response

J. Francis Stafford, D.D.

I found Bishop George's paper very informative and useful. He places in a pastoral context the notion of culture and elaborates upon the relationship of the Catholic Church and culture. In May, 1990, the bishop spoke at our Archdiocesan Convocation on the Laity in Denver; we are still being enriched by his insights on the role of an informed laity in the development of public opinion in Church and society. His paper is equally stimulating today. Helpful also was the clarity of his paper's division into three points.

First, he presented the historical background to the notion of culture as an anthropological concept found in the Church's magisterium.

Second, he developed the ecclesial conversation between faith and culture since Vatican II and its five theological implications. Throughout his paper we find the words "dialogue" and "conversation"; one of his central messages is the importance of developing a conscious awareness of the need for this dialogue at all levels of the Church. His highlighting the importance of dialogue reminds me of the centrality of this concept in Pope Paul VI's first encyclical letter, *Ecclesiam suam*.

The Pope devoted the third part of his letter (which was over half the entire document) to "the dialogue of salvation" between the Church and world, elaborating at length upon the nature of this sacred dialogue. He particularly distinguished it from a Socratic-type dialogue which can be more rationalistic and non-historical in its presuppositions.

Third, Bishop George showed the pastoral implications of this dialogue between faith and culture. Catholic missionaries need to reflect systematically in each stage of the missionary endeavor with constant reference to anthropology and theology. The bishop then described the six ecclesial stages of growth to maturity.

The understanding of "culture" in the documents of the Second Vatican Council seems rooted more in the secular etymology of the word, "a piece of tilled land," rather than in its later, more religious but not unrelated, meaning, "cultus"—cult, worship. The dependence of the latter upon the former is seen in William Langland's *Piers Plowman* where he uses the metaphor of a farm-field to describe the Christian life: to possess "half an acre to harrow by the highway."

This two-fold rootedness of the word "culture" in secular and sacred experience highlights my difficulties in coming to grips with this term in an ecclesial context. I am unclear about the implications and consequences of "culture" for pastoral and systematic theology. At best the term seems pretheological, as the use of the related word, "world," is in *Gaudium et spes*. Its technical origins in the discipline of anthropology hint at where the theological concept of culture is to be defined, analyzed, and encountered in the Church, i.e., within the second and third parts of the Creed, in which we declare our faith that the eternal Son of God come down from heaven "for us men" (in Greek, *anthropous*) "and became man" (*anthropos*). It will be within our confession of the incarnation that the term "culture" will acquire further theological weight.

I am also hesitant about what Bishop George identifies as the counciliar foundation for this new dialogue between faith and culture. He indicates that the famous words of Pope John XXIII, repeated by *Gaudium et spes*, are the root-tap of the council's teaching on "culture." "For the deposit and truths of faith are one thing, the manner in expressing them is another" (62). The bishop acknowledges that the criticism of this formula as "rationalistic in light of linguistic theories current today" is justified. It may be worth critiquing further the philosophical underpinnings of this formula in light of Father DiNoia's earlier comments about the relationship of the universal and particular. The distinction made by the council between "the deposit and truths of faith" and "the manner of expressing them" may seem to parallel too closely the German Enlightenment's claim that true reality exists not in an embodied form, but only in a spiritual form.

The most creative Catholic theology of the twentieth century has called the Church away from dependency upon the self-sufficiency of such rationalism. In Vatican II the Church defines herself as utterly dependent for her existence upon the Eucharistic representation of the One Sacrifice of Christ; and consequently she is historically ordered by the covenantal freedom of that "One Flesh." The dialogue between faith and culture should not be founded on an understanding which may lead inadvertently to a dichotomy between the supposedly ineffable truth of doctrine and the consequent relativity of its every concrete historical expression.

Our inability to speak of "culture" with greater theological precision has led to severe strains in missiology and in the evangelization of culture. A recent article illustrates this. In a 1991 Catholic weekly periodical, a missionary priest relates his impressions after reading through the forty-three volumes of the *Jesuit Relations*. He writes, "There was only one page that gave evidence of a human concern that what the missionaries were doing was perhaps not best for the Indians." He continues that "the missionaries helped erode [the Indians'] traditional spirit." He concludes, "On the practical human level, for the American Indian as a whole, it would have been better for them never to have heard of Jesus from Europeans" (Thomas J. Fitzpatrick, S.J., "Being a Missionary," *America* 164 (July 8, 1991) 612).

The priest whose words are quoted above is a son of St. Ignatius of Loyola, the five-hundredth anniversary of whose birth we celebrate this year. How different are the soteriological foundations which motivated the extraordinary apostolic efforts of Ignatius Loyola and the early Jesuits in their mission to call the non-believer to an acceptance of Christ. Rev. Paul J. Mankowski, S.J., in a critique of his confrere, states that Father Fitzpatrick's understanding of culture seems to be that "each culture in our world has a native *genius* or spirit, and Christians who displace this spirit in spreading the Gospel do harm rather than good to the people they evangelize."

In my judgment, it would be more fruitful to ground the dialogue between culture and the Catholic faith upon the teaching of *Dei verbum* (8–10). There we learn that the historical Church is the actual historical subject of the doctrinal tradition. *Dei verbum* effectively bars any possible inference from the above-quoted text from *Gaudium et spes* that doctrine is fundamentally non-historical.

I am insisting that the dialogue should be founded upon a religious rather than a scientific sense of "culture." At the same time we must retrieve the biblical, patristic, and early medieval hermeneutic as the groundwork for a restatement of history in a tridimensional order, as I elaborated upon in my paper this morning.

In concluding, I wish to compare Bishop George's description of the stages of a local Church's growth to maturity with a favorite passage of mine from J. Henry Newman.

Bishop George elaborates the six stages in the following way:

1. A pre-evangelization study of a particular living culture needs to be done in relationship to the primary images of the Christian faith.

2. A first proclamation of the gospel calls forth a new and small community of Christians. While catechesis continues, the newly baptized experience new relationships among themselves.

3. The primary images of the Christian faith continue to modify and purify the relationships within this nascent Church. Greater awareness of the communion between the maturing Church and the universal Church is experienced.

4. A stage is reached within this local Church where it is possible to have theological reflection upon the Christian community's life and worship.

5. The members of the local Church become more conscious of the need of the transformation of their own culture in the light of the gospel.

6. The local Church is now prepared to be in mission to proclaim Jesus as Lord.

Cardinal Newman saw a similar development of a nascent Church in seventh-century Europe. The sons of St. Benedict had begun the evangelization of the continent. Here is Newman's description.

"Benedict found the world, physical and social, in ruins, and his mission was to restore it in the way, not of science, but of nature, not as if setting out to do it, not professing to do it by any set time or by any rare specific or by any series of strokes, but so quietly, patiently, gradually, that often, till the work was done, it was not known to be doing. It was a restoration, rather than a visitation, correction or conversion. The new world he helped to create was a growth rather than a structure. Silent men were observed about the country, or discovered in the forest, digging, clearing, and building; and other silent men, not seen were sitting in the cold cloister, tiring their eyes and keeping their attention on the stretch, while they painfully deciphered and copied and recopied the manuscript which they had saved. There was no one that 'contended, or cried out,' or drew attention to what was going on; but by degrees the woody swamp became a hermitage, a religious house, a farm, an abbey, a village, a seminary, a school of learning, and a city. Roads and bridges connected it with other abbeys and cities, which had similarly grown up" ("The Mission of St. Benedict" in *Essays and Sketches*, ed. Charles Frederick Harrold [New York: Longmans, Green and Co., 1948] 273-74).

Newman says that the object of the Benedictine evangelization of early Europe was "the world, physical and social"; this appears to be our understanding of what is called "culture." The ministers of cultural evangelization, the monks, were not conscious of themselves as agents of change; their mission was one of restoration (cf. Eph 1), not by way of science, but of nature. It should also be noted that their missionary work was a growth rather than a structure—a favorite theme in Newman's theology of development of doctrine. *Lectio divina* of Sacred Scriptures was the foundation of the restoration of what God intended "in the beginning" rather than the scientific *quaerens* which characterized the later schools. It was a recapitulation in and by Christ of the original unity of man. Such is the task of every evangelization of culture.

IV

The Church and Dialogue with Other Religions
A Plea for the Recognition of Differences

Joseph Augustine DiNoia, O.P.

In an important recent essay entitled "The End of Dialogue," British theologian John Milbank challenges many of the assumptions underlying Christian talk about interreligious dialogue.[1] Although targeted specifically at the pluralist theology of religions exemplified by *The Myth of Christian Uniqueness* (edited by John Hick and Paul Knitter),[2] Milbank's remarks can be read as having a wider reference.

The burden of Milbank's thesis is that our talk about interreligious dialogue regularly embodies a covertly westernizing and Christianizing approach to non-Western cultural and religious traditions. Indeed, he asserts, the very "terms of discourse which provide both the favored categories for encounter with other religions—*dialogue, pluralism*, and the like—together with the criteria for acceptable limits of the pluralist embrace—social justice, liberation, and so forth—are themselves embedded in a wider Western discourse become globally dominant."[3] Arguing that the category of "religion" itself imposes Western conceptions on the complex social institutions of other cultures, he states that "what we are often talking about when we speak of the religious, are the basic organizing categories for an entire culture: the

---

1. John Milbank, "The End of Dialogue," in *Christian Uniqueness Reconsidered*, ed. Gavin D'Costa (Maryknoll: Orbis Books, 1990) 175. This essay should be read in light of Milbank's important recent book, *Theology and Social Theory* (Oxford: Basil Blackwell, 1990)

2. John Hick and Paul Knitter, eds., *The Myth of Christian Uniqueness* (Maryknoll: Orbis Books, 1987).

3. Milbank, "The End of Dialogue," 175.

images, word-forms, and practices which specify 'what there is' for a particular society."[4]

Milbank suggests further that the very supposition of the possibility of dialogue is a questionable one. For the notion of dialogue projects an ideal of cooperative rational inquiry directed to the attainment of truth concerning an agreed upon subject on the basis of some commonly accepted starting point. In fact, he contends, no such agreement or common basis exist. Milbank argues persuasively that even dialogue inspired by apparently religiously neutral commitments to social justice and liberation presupposes Western secularized conceptions of politics and legality. He concludes that "the moment of contemporary recognition of other cultures and religions . . . is itself . . . none other than the moment of the total obliteration of other cultures by Western norms and categories, with their freight of Christian influence."[5]

I cannot do full justice to Milbank's complex argument in this relatively brief presentation. Nor can I do any more than note in passing the degree to which his observations are confirmed by some Jewish, Muslim, Hindu, and Buddhist reactions to Christian-initiated dialogues. A selection of these can be found in Stanley J. Samartha's helpful survey, *One Christ—Many Religions*.[6]

What I can do is take John Milbank's challenge seriously. The Church has announced a "firm and irreversible" commitment to dialogue.[7] Does the enactment of this commitment inevitably entail the blurring or, in Milbank's terms, the Christianizing of the profile of alien religious and cultural traditions? I shall argue that it need not, provided that engagement in dialogue can be theologically justified in ways that take account of the distinctiveness and integrity of other religious traditions. It is in this sense that my remarks on this occasion can be taken as a "plea for the recognition of differences" in Christian relations with other religious people.[8] While, as we shall see, much of

---

4. Ibid., 177.

5. Ibid., 175.

6. Stanley J. Samartha, *One Christ—Many Religions* (Maryknoll: Orbis Books, 1991), 13–31. See also Paul J. Griffiths, *Christianity through Non-Christian Eyes* (Maryknoll: Orbis Books, 1991).

7. "Dialogue and Proclamation: Reflections and Orientations on Interreligious Dialogue and the Proclamation of the Gospel of Jesus Christ," paragraph 54, *Origins* 21 (1991) 130.

8. The phrase is drawn from Steven Katz, "Language, Epistemology and Mysticism," in *Mysticism and Philosophical Analysis*, ed. Steven T. Katz (New York: Oxford University Press, 1978) 25.

the recent debate has been concerned to reconcile dialogue with mission, Milbank's paper turns our attention to a new problematic whose outlines are only just beginning to be discernible. The Christian commitment to interreligious dialogue, far from entailing the "obliteration of other cultures" (*pace* Milbank), logically presupposes a willingness to take the distinctive features of other religious traditions seriously. The Church has not yet grasped the full significance of this implication of its embrace of interreligious dialogue.

In these pages, I will first endeavor to define the contours of the new problematic. Then, I will suggest elements of a resolution that is compatible with the results achieved by the magisterium in its struggle to resolve the earlier problematic of dialogue and mission.

1) Mission and Dialogue: The Problematic

First we need to develop a perspective on the gradual appropriation and endorsement of the concept and project of interreligious dialogue on the part of the magisterium.

The remote origins of the religious use of the notion of dialogue lie in the work of existentialist and personalist thinkers in the first quarter of this century, notably Martin Buber, whose enormously influential book, *I and Thou,* appeared in 1923. But it was only after World War II, according to Eric Sharpe, that the notion came to be applied to interreligious relations.[9] To be sure, interreligious conversations have had a very long history. But, for a variety of reasons, such contacts have been more actively pursued since the early twentieth century. The discrediting and collapse of colonial empires spelled the resurgence of non-Western cultures and religions. Particularly in those former colonies that lie within the ambit of major religious traditions (like Islam, Buddhism, and Hinduism), the missionary enterprise found itself forced to adopt an increasingly defensive posture. Sharpe asserts that "it was in this atmosphere that the word *dialogue* began to emerge as the only workable term with which to describe the proper attitude of one group of believers over against another."[10]

At the outset, the term "dialogue" and the stance it represents were championed principally by liberal Christians. Conservatives, according to Sharpe, "found the term unacceptable, since it implicitly placed religious traditions on a par with one another, or at least was less than ex-

---

9. Eric J. Sharpe, "Dialogue of Religions," *Encyclopedia of Religions* 4:344.
10. Ibid.

plicit when it came to affirming the claims of Christianity."[11] But since the mid-twentieth century, and particularly over the past twenty-five years, the notion of interreligious dialogue has steadily gained in legitimacy within mainstream Christianity. It is commonplace to note that the Second Vatican Council's Declaration on the Church's Relation to Non-Christian Religions (*Nostra aetate*) marked a decisive moment in this legitimation.[12]

But the council's embrace of a dialogical attitude to other religions by no means dispelled the tension—logically speaking—that such an embrace involved for the Christian faith and ethos. This tension was present in the use of the term "dialogue" to describe Christian relations with other religions from very start, and the council did nothing to dispel it. How the appropriation and endorsement of interreligious dialogue could be consistent with a commitment to the mission *ad gentes* was not specified. Vatican II in effect simply juxtaposed the commitments to mission and to dialogue without undertaking to show how, doctrinally speaking, they could be reconciled with one another. This task was bequeathed to the magisterium and to subsequent theological reflection.

Much of the debate in the aftermath of the council has been devoted to this issue. Does engagement in dialogue and the attitudes it entails undercut or support a commitment to the proclamation of the gospel? A voluminous theological literature attests to the variety and ingenuity of the strategies that have been deployed in pursuit of a satisfactory answer to this question.[13]

Within the perspective of an evolution that spans much of this century, the significance of two recent documents of the Holy See stands out sharply. In both documents, resolving the underlying tension between mission and dialogue remains fundamental.

The encyclical *Redemptoris missio* resolves the tension by its forthright subsumption of dialogue within or under mission. This marks an important development in the way the Church understands its participation in interreligious dialogue. Among the activities of the mission *ad gentes*, dialogue is listed along with proclamation and witness as

11. Ibid. For a fuller discussion, see Eric J. Sharpe, *Comparative Religion: A History* (New York: Charles Scribner's Sons, 1975) 251–66.

12. Though it is not within the scope of this paper to discuss this, it should be noted that the council's initiative in this regard had an important impact on policies subsequently adopted by the World Council of Churches.

13. For bibliography, see Jacques Dupuis, *Jesus Christ at the Encounter of World Religions* (Maryknoll: Orbis Books, 1991).

one of the "paths of mission" presented in chapter 5 of the encyclical. At one stroke, the encyclical combines a strong reaffirmation of the Church's commitment to mission with a clear endorsement of participation in interreligious dialogue.

The second document is the product, significantly, of both the Pontifical Council for Interreligious Dialogue and the Congregation for the Evangelization of Peoples. This Vatican paper on "Dialogue and Proclamation" follows the lead of *Redemptoris missio*.[14] In its thorough rehearsal of developments since the council, the paper clearly regards the tension implicit in the commitments to mission and dialogue as an issue of fundamental importance. Its resolution parallels that of *Redemptoris missio* when it asserts that "proclamation and dialogue are . . . component elements and authentic forms of the one evangelizing mission of the church."[15]

The importance of these two documents cannot be overestimated. In light of the history of the concept of dialogue over the past century, these documents represent what might be called the complete "domestication" of the previously alien or at least marginal notion of dialogue within the catholic mainstream. From having been a maverick concept less than fifty years ago, interreligious dialogue has now become "an integral element of the church's evangelizing mission."[16]

2) Mission and Dialogue: Doctrinal Resolution

Let us consider now the "doctrinal logic" of this appropriation and endorsement of interreligious dialogue. If my reading of the history of this development is correct, then the central problematic has been defined by the effort to reconcile the embrace of dialogue with the commitment to mission.

Subsequent doctrinal development and theological reflection have capitalized on a move basic to the logic of *Nostra aetate*. This declaration framed its legitimation of interreligious dialogue in terms of an appreciation of the implicitly Christian elements discernible within other religious traditions. On this view, the basis required for dialogue lies in these commonly shared though implicit elements, and the object of dialogue is to bring these elements to light.

Over the quarter century since the promulgation of *Nostra aetate*, it

---

14. "Dialogue and Proclamation" makes this connection explicit.
15. Ibid., paragraph 2.
16. Ibid., paragraph 38.

has become increasingly clear that latent precisely in this cluster of premises was the possibility of reconciling participation in dialogue with commitment to mission. Thus, it eventuated that the magisterium, and theologians as well, sought to resolve the tension between mission and dialogue by appeal to a set of doctrinal resources that can be seen to warrant *both* mission *and* dialogue.

The argument runs something like this: The single purpose of the triune God in creation and redemption is to bring the whole human race into communion with the Trinity and in this way to consummate its unity as God's family. The principal agent of this divine purpose is the Son, in whose image all are created and in whose blood all are redeemed. This purpose continues to be actively pursued in history by the Holy Spirit at work through the Church which proclaims "God's wisdom, mysterious, hidden, which God predetermined before the ages for our glory" (1 Cor 2:7) and affords access to the riches of Christ's grace. The Church's mission is to proclaim this purpose to the ends of the earth. In the course of pursuing this mission, the Church understands that the Spirit is at work in the hearts of all human beings and that through the Spirit all are called to fellowship with God in the blood of Christ. Hence, the Church must suppose that, in the course of the mission *ad gentes*, the Spirit's presence and action will in principle be recognizable. Moreover, the mission will in part consist in bringing this presence and action to light in the minds of those to whom it is directed. Christian respect for the values enshrined in other religious traditions arises from these convictions about the universal scope of God's activity in inviting human persons into communion with himself and with each other in him. This respect in turn impels Christians to engage in dialogue with persons who, while they do not share explicit Christian faith, must be supposed to be touched by the Spirit and striving according to their lights to respond to this grace, although they do not know this. It is in this complex sense that dialogue can be said to be integral to the Church's evangelizing mission: mission and dialogue express the single, though differentiated, Christian participation in the single, though diversely advanced, purpose of the triune God.

Within the limits of the dialogue and mission problematic, and because the problematic posed by the encounter of Christians with other religious people is defined chiefly in these terms, this pattern of argument is brilliantly successful. Indeed, it can be read as actually required by fundamental Christian doctrines. If one's objective is to show that for sound doctrinal reasons and not simply for strategic ones engagement in dialogue is not incompatible with mission, it is then appropriate to appeal chiefly to specifically Christian motivations for this engagement. It is consequently appropriate to affirm that in dialogue one seeks to discover the truth that the Spirit plants in the dialogue partner. The doctrinal legitimation for dialogue consists in exploiting dialogue's potential for the identification, explicitation, and realization of the Christian virtualities present in the other. Just as the determination to join in the work of the Holy Spirit impels the Christian to engage in mission, so respect for the universal presence and action of the Holy Spirit encourages the Christian to participate in interreligious dialogue.

The discussion of interreligious dialogue in *Redemptoris missio* exhibits this pattern of argument in what I shall call a doctrinally modest form of inclusivism. This is an inclusivism that is entailed by central Christian doctrines. As Christoph Schwöbel puts it,

> no theological understanding of the religions can be adequate which implicitly or expressly denies the all-encompassing presence of God for his creation and which calls the universality of God's will of love for his creation into question. . . . The religions therefore have to be seen as human responses to God's all encompassing presence and activity in which God is active in all forms of created being as the ground of being and meaning and as the source and end of its fulfillment.[17]

The Vatican paper "Dialogue and Proclamation" represents an amplification of the sketch outlined in the encyclical. To this extent, the paper begins to display some of the features of what I shall call a radical or fullblown theological inclusivism. This form of inclusivism is apparent in the work of inclusivist theologians like Jacques Dupuis.[18]

What distinguishes this fullblown theological inclusivism from the doctrinally modest inclusivism of the encyclical is the endeavor, not simply to show the compatibility of dialogue with mission, but to field an entire interpretive framework for the understanding and assessment of other religious and cultural traditions. It is at this point that the difficulties identified by Milbank begin to appear in stark outline.

In its fullblown theological form, the pattern of argument outlined above serves as the basis for applying nearly the entire apparatus used to structure our understanding of the Christian faith to our understanding of other religions. The categories of revelation, sacred scrip-

---

17. Christoph Schwöbel, "Particularity, Universality and the Religions," in D'Costa, *Christian Uniqueness*, 39.
18. See especially his recent book cited in note 13 above.

ture, salvation, grace, worship of God, moral life, and so on, are introduced as supportive of a positive evaluation of other religions even when such categories are completely inapplicable to them or applicable only in qualified senses. The distinctive strands of other religious traditions, woven into the integral fabric of their particular doctrinal schemes, are never permitted to emerge in the clarity of their intractable otherness.

Consider the example of Buddhism. It is a matter of dispute whether it should even be termed a religion, but be that as it may. In its various forms, Buddhism is in the main non-theistic and cannot be said to possess the concept of a presently existing object of worship upon whom life is focused. It makes little sense to speak of Buddhist traditions as originating in a revelation since there is no transcendent agent to reveal itself. It follows that Buddhist sacred books cannot be thought to be inspired. Indeed, it is a matter of considerable importance to Buddhists to assert just the opposite about their sacred books, since the wisdom they contain is understood to be, not a transcendent communication, but the outcome of reflection on experience by Gautama the Buddha. By definition these books are consequently accessible to anyone who can follow his line of reasoning.

For Buddhism, the ultimate aim of life is not any kind of present or future union with an existing object but the enjoyment of a state beyond selfhood. For the achievement of this state, especially in the view of Theravada Buddhists, reliance on the assistance of transcendent grace is most definitely not required and the expectation of such assistance can be positively harmful. Whatever may be the value of love and compassion in earthly life, the realization of these virtues is by no means constitutive of the enlightened "life" which is the object of striving for the Buddhist.

I have offered some Buddhist illustrations in order to exhibit some contrasts between distinctive Buddhist doctrines and the Christian scheme. Persons familiar with other major religious traditions could undoubtedly contribute more examples to the list. I do not suggest that these illustrations represent clearly defined doctrinal oppositions between Buddhist and Christian traditions.[19] My point is far simpler. These contrasts, and others that could be cited, suggest that significant elements of the Buddhist scheme are difficult to reconstrue in the terms provided by the Christian scheme.

For the purposes of dialogue, it would be desirable to seek an un-

---

19. On this complex issue, see William A. Christian, *Oppositions of Religious Doctrines* (New York: Seabury Press, 1972).

derstanding of the larger doctrinal setting of particular elements of the belief and practice of Buddhist as well as of other major religious traditions. Common versions of fullblown theological inclusivism in effect erase the particularities of other traditions by viewing them chiefly in the cognate terms of the Christian scheme. Armed with a theology of religions in this vein, one approaches interreligious dialogue with the expectation that one will discover, not something intractably other, but a pale reflection of oneself. In effect, independently of their transmutation to a Christian grid, the distinctive features of other religious traditions are rendered virtually invisible.

We have seen that the modest doctrinal inclusivism of *Redemptoris missio* provides a powerful legitimation for participation in interreligious dialogue viewed as essential to the mission *ad gentes*. For some theologians, this doctrinally required inclusivism opens the way to the sort of Christianizing account of other religious traditions that fails to acknowledge the distinctiveness and integrity of other religious schemes as serious alternatives.

But the encyclical need not be read as warranting only this kind of development. If, as I have argued, the encyclical set its sights primarily on the dialogue and mission problematic, it need not be read as providing the kind of detailed blueprint for assessing other religions that is typical of fullblown theological inclusivism. On the contrary, there is every reason to suppose that the encyclical invites us to move toward a newly emerging problematic. Given its forceful confirmation of the Christian aptness of engagement in interreligious dialogue, the encyclical invites us to consider what this engagement entails.

3) Interreligious Dialogue: The New Problematic

From a world historical perspective, the Christian espousal of interreligious dialogue represents a realistic assessment of and an adaptation to the new situation facing the Church in its encounter with the major religions. In the past Christian mission met with most of its success among peoples of traditional or local religions. But as its focus shifts increasingly to the adherents of major religious traditions, the context of mission alters dramatically.

John Milbank notes a commonplace, though with particular insight, when he states that:

> every major religion is *already* the result of a confronting of the fact of religious differences and an attempt to subsume such differences. . . . By comparison, genuinely local religions . . . may scarcely have had to

confront the question of whether their beliefs and practices are relevant beyond the confines of their own society; this is presumably why they are so liable to conversion by or accommodation within the terms of a major religion, which is in part the result of such a confrontation. The major religions are notoriously not so susceptible to conversion or accommodation, precisely because they already embody a more abstract, universal, deterritorialized cultural framework, although they do not usually succumb to the temptation of trying to found this universality in a reason independent of all particularized memory.[20]

Although Milbank does not mean to draw this conclusion, his remarks can be taken to imply that it is only through interreligious dialogue that Christians can relate to the major religions and in this way realize the Church's evangelizing mission in the context of societies within their ambits. This recognition does not represent simply a strategic redirection of missionary energies, but, as the theological justification for dialogue indicates, a recovery of the unimpeachably traditional doctrines of the universal salvific will of God and the universal scope of the action and presence of the Holy Spirit. The need to adapt missionary strategies to a new situation may be regarded as the providential occasion for the retrieval and reaffirmation of truths latent in and, to be fair, never far beneath the surface of the doctrinal and theological traditions of Christianity.

In order to grasp something of what the espousal of dialogue entails in the present circumstances, we need some account of the nature of interreligious dialogue. The term can designate a variety of things. As Eric Sharpe has noted: "One is sometimes almost forced to reflect that the cause of sympathetic inter-religious dialogue might be better served if the word were to be laid aside for a time. . . . [W]hen a single word can be used in such diverse senses, and serve the interests of attitudes involving distinctively different presuppositions (rational and non-rational), clearly some semantic tidying up is necessary."[21]

The forms of dialogue with which Christians have become familiar, that is interconfessional dialogue and dialogue with modern thinkers, are in marked contrast to the situation posed by interreligious dialogue. Here, the Church confronts, not disagreements arising from a fundamentally shared faith, or from secular philosophical critique, but massive and enduring bodies of religious wisdom and highly ramified

20. Milbank, "The End of Dialogue," 180.
21. Eric J. Sharpe, "The Goals of Inter-Religious Dialogue," in *Truth and Dialogue*, ed. John Hick (London: Sheldon Press, 1974) 91.

systems of doctrines derived from sources as ancient and rich as any of her own. The challenges posed by this encounter come not from religiously skeptical individuals but from religious communities advancing well-developed alternative conceptions of the ultimate aim of life and the pattern life ought to have in view of this aim.

Interreligious dialogue is a form of religious interaction in which members of different religious communities engage in conversation about various features of their distinctive traditions and patterns of life. In line with the wide variety of purposes which might be pursued by conversations of this sort, there would be opportunities for a variety of utterances in such settings. Participants might report about the historical development or subtle meanings of some aspects of their traditions. They might offer examples of their communities' prayers or relate events in the lives of their communities' founders or saints. In addition to speaking of such things, the participants would have occasion to mention some of the doctrines of their communities. Given the seriousness with which they view the conversation and the respect with which they regard the other participants, they would have to be prepared to present some reasons for doctrines which, as persons who profess adherence to particular religious traditions, they hold to express true beliefs and right courses of action.

Since there would presumably be disagreements among participants whose communities teach different and possibly conflicting doctrines, those engaged in dialogue would have to acknowledge the distinctiveness of the doctrines presented by other communities represented in the dialogue. Serious recognition of the diversity of religious doctrines would be important at least as an initial state of mind, even if the participants were to conclude at the end of the dialogue that the oppositions among their doctrines were only apparent ones and that at some deeper level the doctrines of their different communities were all consistent with one another.[22]

This description of the logical features of interreligious dialogue suggests that the course of action recommended by the Church in its espousal and encouragement of dialogue is a complex one. This recommendation seems to include at least the following recommendations as well: (1) Christians should respect other dialogue participants both as fellow human beings and as fellow seekers after religious truth; (2) Christians should study and esteem the doctrines of the other religious communities represented in dialogue; (3) Christians engaged in interreligious dialogue should be prepared to propose, de-

---

22. See Christian, *Oppositions*.

velop, and argue for their doctrines; (4) Christians should take notice of the proposals of alien religious claims and the arguments which may be advanced in their behalf by other dialogue participants; (5) Christians should be open to the possible developments of their own doctrines which might be suggested in the course of their study of other religions and in dialogue with their adherents.

If a religious community teaches its members to engage in dialogue it must at least envisage the possibility that its members will have occasion to engage in an interreligious dialogue with the features described above. It is reasonable to assume, therefore, that if it commends dialogue, it also commends the courses of action outlined above.

Someone who recommends participation in dialogue may be unaware that in doing so he or she by implication is recommending other specific courses of action along with it. If for some reason the person cannot accept one of the implied recommendations, it may be necessary to withdraw the recommendation to engage in dialogue or at least to rethink the objectionable item in the series. But unless the contrary is explicitly indicated, it is reasonable to assume that in recommending dialogue a religious community recommends as well the courses of action that flow from it.

By espousing and teaching the policy of dialogue, the Church can be regarded as having envisaged a setting for interreligious dialogue such I have described. It is reasonable to assume that in recommending that its members engage in dialogue with other religions the Church is also teaching the five points presented above.

We have seen that traditional Christian doctrines plainly support the attitudes of respect and esteem supposed by the determination to engage in interreligious dialogue. Faith in God's all-embracing providential care for the human race would seem to require that the Church admit that its own traditions cannot have a monopoly on religious truth and virtue. Charity and justice demand that Christians appreciate the goodness of other religious people, the truth of some of their doctrines about God, the human condition and other matters, the rectitude of their moral codes, the beauty of their ritual, the wisdom of their institutions, and the marvels of their art, literature, and culture. It seems clear that Catholic doctrine could be construed to warrant the respect, esteem, and readiness to study which are commended by the first and second recommendations I have noted.

This supposition seems to be on equally firm ground with regard to the third recommendation. There is no rule which requires Catholic Christians to remain silent about the Church's doctrines in the presence of non-members. On the contrary, they are encouraged to bear witness to their convictions and hope about the salvation which God promises. Hence Christian doctrines can plausibly be supposed to warrant the recommendation that Christians engaged in dialogue be prepared to propose their doctrines and argue for them in ways that will be comprehensible to persons who do not hold them.

Respect for what may be divinely inspired truth present in other religions implies a readiness to entertain the doctrinal proposals which may be advanced in the course of dialogue. Nothing in Christian doctrine can be construed as opposed to noting alien religious claims proposed in the course of dialogue. Furthermore, respect for the truth which may be present in other religions implies a readiness to make it one's own. A willingness to appropriate the truths learned in the course of study and dialogue can be shown to be consistent with Christian doctrines and is in any case well-attested by historical precedents.

It follows that the Church's endorsement of interreligious dialogue entails the readiness to take the distinctive features of other religious traditions seriously. A modest doctrinal inclusivism can be understood to support this readiness and is preferable to the fullblown theological inclusivism that reconstrues alien religious doctrines largely in Christian terms. This point is important even when dialogue is seen primarily as a means of fostering collaboration in socially constructive programs. Christoph Schwöbel remarks that "the possibility of practical cooperation of members of different religious traditions does not depend . . . on a consensus of shared religious justifications. On the contrary, the possibilities of cooperation will be enhanced if both parties are not only permitted but encouraged to find the justification of their participation in shared righteous action in the particular and distinctive perspectives, which are based on the particular disclosure of truth constitutive for each perspective."[23]

4) Conclusion: Inclusivism and Dialogue

In conclusion, allow me to note that the approach to interreligious dialogue sketched here is fully compatible with a strong affirmation of Christian mission. The doctrinally modest inclusivism that views interreligious dialogue as an intrinsic moment of mission remains intact. For the determination on the part of the Church to respect the

---

23. Schwöbel, "Particularity," 45.

claims advanced by other communities in dialogue is paralleled by its own conviction about the universal scope of salvation in Jesus Christ. As Pope John Paul II wrote in *Redemptoris missio*: "While respecting the beliefs and sensitivities of all, we must first clearly affirm our faith in Christ, the one Savior of humanity, a faith we have received as a gift from on high, not as a result of any merit of our own."[24]

The approach advocated here would permit Christian participants in dialogue and Christian missionaries to argue against the aims of life as commended by other communities which inadequately, erroneously, or misguidedly present what the Christian community also strives to commend and foster in fidelity to its risen Lord. Paul Griffiths demonstrates this in his important book, *An Apology for Apologetics*.[25]

The approach suggested here has advantages over radical or fullblown inclusivist positions taken to legitimate the practice of mission. For many inclusivists, the Christian mission is viewed primarily as the identification of virtualities already present in other religions, or as the explicitation and arousal of inclinations already implicit in the dispositions of their adherents. Although the inclusivist theology of mission envisages the correction and fulfillment of non-Christian practices and beliefs, it nonetheless fails to sustain the urgency toward proclamation that traditional Christian doctrines have been understood to entail. It seems clear that the traditional Christian policy of evangelization and mission has something more vigorous in view.

Generally speaking, the inclusivist, not to mention pluralist, approaches to the theology of mission have been unsuccessful at summoning the energies of the Christian communities in which they are dominant for the exercise of mission and evangelization. It is a commonplace to note the contrast of these views of mission with those of communities in which more exclusivist forms of theology of religions predominate. But the argument of this paper suggests that engagement in Christian mission can be fully legitimated by non-exclusivist doctrinal and theological strategies. A vigorous Christian mission presupposes convictions about the particular hope and the universal scope of the salvation to which Christians are charged to bear witness. Esteem for other religious communities and respect for their members

---

24. Paragraph 11.
25. (Maryknoll: Orbis Books, 1991). For a fuller discussion of the issues addressed in this paper, see J. A. DiNoia, *The Diversity of Religions: A Christian Perspective* (Washington, D.C.: The Catholic University of America Press, 1992).

do not preclude engagement in this mission, even if they do entail abandoning many of the practices associated with missionary activity in the past.

* * *

John Milbank has asserted that the Christian espousal of interreligious dialogue contributes to the "obliteration of other cultures by Western norms and categories, with their freight of Christian influence." In this paper, I have suggested that, while there are forms of theological legitimation for the Church's engagement in dialogue that are vulnerable to this critique, it is possible to advance a modest doctrinal inclusivism that not only encourages respect for the distinctiveness and integrity of other religious traditions but entails it.

Response

Avery Dulles, S.J.

In essential agreement with Vatican Council II and the teaching of Pope John Paul II, Father DiNoia presents a theological justification for both interreligious dialogue and missionary proclamation. He traces a certain progress in recent official teaching. Before Vatican II the Church had a theology of proclamation but scarcely of interreligious dialogue. The council approved of dialogue and legitimized it on the ground that Christianity was the fulfillment of the religious intimations and aspirations of the whole human race. The council also held that missionary proclamation was urgent, but it failed to explain the relationship between the two forms of encounter. In *Nostra aetate*, Father DiNoia explains, the two are simply juxtaposed. He credits the present Pope with a major advance. In his encyclical *Redemptoris missio* John Paul II integrates dialogue into the larger concept of mission or evangelization, and shows how both dialogue and proclamation are authentic forms of evangelization.

With all of this I can only agree. Although dialogue and proclamation are distinct forms of activity, they are, as the Pope states, reciprocally linked together. On the one hand, any serious religious dialogue must contain an element of proclamation, because the participants are expected to profess and defend their own beliefs. Nothing in the nature of dialogue requires the participants to bracket or conceal their differences. They must, however, state their convictions in a civil manner, with openness to being questioned, and listen to the other participants with respect and readiness to learn. On the other hand, dialogue enters into the process of proclamation, for it enables the interlocutors to gain a better understanding of each other's mentality, and thereby equips them to proclaim more effectively.

On these central points I suspect that Father DiNoia and I agree with each other and, I trust, with the Pope. But I should like to examine in greater detail the way in which Father DiNoia explains the relationship between the faiths that are in dialogue. He speaks of exclusivism and inclusivism, and within the latter he distinguishes between "fullblown inclusivism" and "doctrinally modest inclusivism." His own position, as we might expect, is the last-named, for who would wish to be anything but doctrinally modest?

Some of my difficulties at this point have to do with terminology. Terms such as "inclusivism" and "exclusivism," to the best of my knowledge, do not appear in official Church teaching. Although much used in comparative religion, the terms are in my opinion unhelpful, at least unless it is specified what is being included in, or excluded from, what else. As Christians we may surely affirm that the Word of God and the Holy Spirit are at work among all peoples and presumably in all religions, but I would hesitate to say that these other religions are "included" in Christianity. The terminology sounds terribly imperialistic. Possibly the meaning is that whatever is true and salvific in these religions can find a place in Christianity. If so, I agree with the meaning but I have some doubts about the aptness of the terminology.

The problem becomes more complicated when Father DiNoia distinguishes between two forms of inclusivism: fullblown and doctrinally modest. He paraphrases Vatican II and the encyclical *Redemptoris missio* at some length to illustrate what he calls the "brilliantly successful" pattern of argument for the presence of "Christian virtualities" in non-Christian religions. All human beings, he says, are created in the image of God and redeemed by the blood of Christ. The Holy Spirit is at work in the hearts of all, calling them to the same eternal destiny. Christians, then, enter the dialogue with the expectation of finding that their partners, even without knowing it, have been touched by the grace of the Holy Spirit and have been striving to respond to it.

This line of argument, which Father DiNoia attributes to Vatican II and the present Pope, exemplifies the "doctrinally modest form of inclusivism."

How does this differ from the "fullblown" inclusivism that Father DiNoia rejects? The latter, he holds, fails to take the distinctive features of other religions seriously. It regards them as pale reflections of Christianity, and presumes that they can be adequately understood through the categories of Christian theology. These defects, if they were characteristic of the school, would indicate to my mind that their inclusivism was not genuinely dialogic. But Jacques Dupuis, whom Father DiNoia presents as a fullblown inclusivist, insists that openness to the other and readiness to learn are essential to dialogue. Possibly Father DiNoia disagrees when Dupuis goes on to say that a Christian theology of the religions must adhere to the creeds and dogmas of the Church. If there is a disagreement on this point I think I would have to side with Father Dupuis.

As an example of the perilous slip from doctrinally modest to fullblown inclusivism Father DiNoia draws a contrast between *Redemptoris missio*, which wins his approval, and the Vatican paper on "Dialogue and Proclamation," in which he finds features of "fullblown theological inclusivism." So far as I can see, this second document faithfully reproduces the teaching of Vatican II and the present Pope. Far from reducing all other religions to Christianity, it says that dialogue should be aimed at mutual enrichment (par. 9), that Christians in dialogue should allow themselves to be questioned (par. 32), and that they must be prepared to find elements incompatible with Christianity in the other religions (par. 31). Thus the positions taken in the paper on "Dialogue and Proclamation" would seem to fit the description of doctrinal modesty.

Father DiNoia seeks to clarify his distinction between the two forms of inclusivism by his treatment of the categories to be used in interreligious dialogue. At one stage he points out the inadequacy of categories such as "revelation, sacred scripture, salvation, grace, worship of God, moral life, and so on" (p. 128), at least for Buddhist-Christian dialogue. To use these categories, he holds, would show a failure to appreciate what is distinctive in the other religion. Somewhat later Father DiNoia proposes that the dialogue participants should take as themes their respective traditions, their forms of prayer, their saints, their doctrines, and the reasons they have for thinking that their doctrines "express true beliefs and right courses of action" (p. 133). I confess that I cannot see why this second set of categories (namely, tradition, prayer, saints, doctrines, and apologetics) is necessarily more respectful of the distinctiveness of other faiths than the first.

To establish any set of categories unilaterally would be contrary to the spirit of genuine dialogue. It is to be expected that the participants themselves will seek together for common categories and common language so that communication may be unimpeded. For some dialogues categories such as scripture, salvation, and worship might prove as helpful and appropriate as prayer, saints, and doctrine. In any case I do not see why the first set of categories should be rejected as "fullblown inclusivism" and the second approved as "doctrinally modest."

As a final argument against "fullblown inclusivism" Father DiNoia maintains that it fails to sustain the urgency of Christian missionary proclamation. This may be true of certain authors who speak of "anonymous Christians" as though one could, without being evangelized, possess the full substance of Christianity, lacking only the name. But a word of caution may be in order. The most vociferous opponents of missionary activity are pluralists who extol the distinctiveness of all religions as though conversion to Christ were always a betrayal. They fear that Christianity, convinced of its own superiority, aims at obliterating the other faiths.

The inclusivist theory offers a defense against this charge. Inclusivists hold that whatever is good and salutary in every religion can find a place in Christianity, which is the fulfillment rather than the abolition of the world's religions. Father DiNoia, upholding the irreducible distinctiveness of the other religions, takes a different approach. But the brevity of his exposition leaves some questions, at least in my mind. Does he insist on this distinctiveness because he esteems and wishes to preserve it or because he thinks that it needs to be overcome? In maintaining that it grounds the urgency of Christian proclamation he implies that it ought to be eliminated. Although Father DiNoia deplores obliterationism in his theory of dialogue, his theology of proclamation could be seen as obliterationist. I should like to hear a fuller exposition of his views on this point.

Missionary Issues in a World Church
A Reflective Synthesis

Joan Frances Gormley, S.S.M.W.

To the disciples who had been with him during his ministry Jesus, after his death and resurrection, gave the solemn charge: "Go, therefore, and make disciples of all nations, baptizing them in the name of the Father, and of the Son, and of the Holy Spirit, teaching them to observe all that I have commanded you" (Matt 28:19-20). Those who had received freely were sent to give freely (Matt 10:8). This pattern at the beginning of the Church's life has been repeated right down to our own day: the light of faith has been handed on person to person and generation to generation, and those who receive it are challenged in their turn to go forth and share with others the riches given them. Thus is the Church and every Christian missionary.

A look at the beginnings of the tradition in which we are rooted can help us understand our place in the Church in this time and place as we ponder the meaning of our participation in Christ's mission of salvation and can also show where we go from here.

The world confronted by the first Christians was a pagan world, grown old in sin and grievously afflicted by every kind of immorality: the breakdown of the family, abortion, infanticide, slavery, war, to mention only a few. Into that aged world, plummeting toward destruction, came men and women bearing the message of victory over death and life in Jesus Christ. These people, truly young in that before them lay the promise of unending life in Christ Jesus, initiated a total revolution and transformation of the societies in which they lived. They regarded Christ as the Truth illuminating every human reality and engaging and fulfilling all the dimensions of the human person. It would not be wrong to apply to many of those early Christians words used to describe one of them, the second-century Christian philosopher and martyr, Justin. One historian writes of him that Justin wanted to make the fire burning in his heart burn in the world. He believed that God would hold accountable those who, once enlightened by the light of Christ, did not testify in favor of the truth. Through the efforts of such men and women, the Christian gospel was planted, matured, and bore fruit in a rich and beautiful culture.

The world of today is not terribly different from the one encountered by the first Christians as they obeyed the Lord's missionary charge. In many ways, our world too is old and worn out by its capitulation to evil, its dulling and deformation of consciences, its covenant with sin and death. The moral ills which plagued the Roman world of the first Christian centuries also afflict the world today. All who have received that message full of fire, which is the gospel of Jesus Christ, are charged with the task of living it in a clear and visible way and passing on the treasure received. For as we have heard many times since the Second Vatican Council, and have heard proclaimed in solemn and urgent terms by the Pope in his encyclical, *Redemptoris missio*, the Church is by nature missionary, and every Christian, in virtue of baptism, shares in that missionary vocation. Our attempts to reflect on the Church's mission to preach the gospel are a way of responding to the Lord's missionary charge to go to the ends of the earth; they place us in the ranks of the earliest missionaries and their successors down to the present.

Standing as we do at the threshold of a new millennium, we encounter questions and difficulties in carrying out the mission that arise from our own time. Some of these we have considered during these days. I would like, in this concluding reflective session, to review the problems set before us by our speakers, as well as the solutions that each proposes. Then I will propose some thoughts for further reflection in the time ahead.

With Father Dulles, we began by considering various positions on the Church's relationship to the kingdom. The New Testament, no more than the Old Testament which influenced it, did not provide a univocal definition of "kingdom" nor a clear statement of the relationship between it and the Church. In Jesus' use of the term, one finds paradoxical, even apparently contradictory ways of looking at the kingdom. It is future; it is present. It is in heaven; it is here in our midst. It is God or Christ ruling; it is the people ruled. It comes from outside history; it comes in the heart of the individual believer. What is to be done with such an elusive concept? Ephrem the Syrian sang about the pearl to which the Lord compared the kingdom, rejoicing at the many images which he saw reflected in it as he turned it over in his hand. Some systematic theologians try to be more rational about the meaning of the kingdom and to solve the problem in such a way that the kingdom is one thing or another. Pannenberg, Küng, and McBrien are examples of the more or less secularizing approach most frequently taken in our time. So strongly do they stress the eschatological aspect of the kingdom that they dissociate it from the Church, which they see to be of this world, a human organization whose task is to serve the kingdom by contributing to the humanization of the world. The Church is seen by them to have no necessary role in the coming of the kingdom. The magisterium, on the other hand, right up to the latest encyclical letter on the missions, has insisted on the close relationship of Church and kingdom—not one of identity to be sure, but one in which the Church and the kingdom are intimately related and in which the Church is, by God's will, necessary for the coming of the kingdom. The Church's proclamation of Christ prepares for the kingdom by uniting men and women with him in whom the kingdom is already present. Once converted and living in Christ, believers share in the work of bringing about the kingdom of God.

A second related question concerns the Church's role in salvation. Is it necessary for salvation? Some contemporary theologians, among them Francis Sullivan, S.J., argue that in saying that "the Church of Christ *subsists in* the Roman Catholic Church," Vatican II was placing the Church of Rome next to other Christian Churches in the manner of a denomination. Archbishop Stafford insisted in his paper on the importance of the recognition of the Church's necessary role in the salvation of humanity, even while we also hold that God's will is for the salvation of all. Alongside his discussion of the Church's necessary role in salvation, Archbishop Stafford also directed attention to the estrangement of many in the United States, as evidenced in the decline of the number of priests, religious, and Catholic institutions, and in the decline in the number attending Mass and receiving the sacrament of reconciliation. The question naturally arises as to whether those leaving perceive the Church as having a necessary role in salvation. We might even push the question further and ask whether there is any deep sense of a need for salvation.

With Bishop George's talk, our attention was turned to those who are being evangelized and specifically to the question of the Church's meeting with the various cultures in missionary lands. He noted the council's optimism about human culture and concern that the Church truly be planted in the soil of the people whom she is evangelizing.

The Church, in proclaiming the gospel of Jesus Christ, does not impose a particular culture on those receiving the proclamation. With this in mind, Bishop George outlined the stages of an inculturated evangelization, beginning from a preparatory study of the meaning of biblical symbols in the receiving culture, and continuing through formation of a small group of converts who remain in the dominant culture and eventually come to the point of doing theology and finding a way of life which is truly their own Christian culture.

Finally, Father DiNoia considered another aspect of the work of evangelization, namely the encounter with world religions. For this aspect of the missionary effort, dialogue is an important tool. Father DiNoia disagrees with the view of John Milbank who says that Christians cannot really engage in dialogue with those of other faiths because they are always seeking to impose their own faith and see themselves as having nothing to learn from the dialogue partner. Father DiNoia, speaking against this view, argues for what he terms a "doctrinally modest form of inclusivism" which would not impose Christian categories on non-Christian religions but would seek to discover them as religions in their own right. Father DiNoia describes the stages in which such a dialogue might be carried out and in which the Christian partner would also have the opportunity for bearing witness to his or her faith.

In summarizing, I have tried merely to present the line of argument of each of our speakers. Now I will try to show points of convergence which seem especially important and then offer some brief concluding reflections.

To begin with, each speaker mentioned the uniqueness of the person of Christ in the work of universal salvation. Christ makes the kingdom present; he is the Savior of all; he is the Word for whose coming the Spirit prepares the hearts of all; with him, the Christian enters into conversation and experiences the heart set afire (Luke 24:32). The Christian proclamation was a call from the witnesses who had seen and heard and touched the Word of Life, Jesus Christ, and wanted to announce him so that others too might enter into fellowship with him and with the Father and thus have life (1 John 1:1-4). The meeting with the Lord is a matter of life and death. Where would we be without him? If our answer is that we can get along quite well, we shall never be impelled to announce him to others. Paul tells the Corinthians that he had determined to speak nothing among them but Jesus Christ and him crucified (1 Cor 2:2); he tells the Galatians that if he comes with any other message than the gospel of Christ, they should not listen to him (Gal 1:8). The missionary, whether in the evangelization of those of other cultures or in the new evangelization of those at home, must truly live in union with Jesus Christ. Otherwise any words will ring less than true. The insight that we should not impose anything extraneous to the gospel on those of other cultures is a good one. Better still is the insight that we cannot neglect the preaching of Jesus Christ. In the early liturgy, the Church prayed for the coming of the kingdom in those words full of longing: "Come, Lord Jesus" (Rev 22:20). We watch with head held high for the coming of the kingdom, even in the midst of the disasters brought on by the fall of the kingdoms of the earth, because we will see the Lord in all his glory (Luke 21:27-28).

A second point of convergence in the four talks was the place of the Church in the missionary task and in the role of offering salvation and holiness to all. This is done, not in the abstract, but in the concrete community, the *koinonia* established by the immersion of each one in Christ. That communion of the faithful is meant to be a visible sign before all of Christ and his victory over sin and death. When the Church is inculturated, it is always through a community which is planted in some part of the creation where it lives the life of Christ and thus builds up the kingdom of God. The witness of the Christian community is thus the first missionary task. Of the members of the community, Paul says that "all of us, gazing on the Lord's glory with unveiled face, are being transformed from glory to glory into his very image by the Lord who is the Spirit." Such transformation is meant to be visible in every aspect of the individual's life and in the corporate life of the body. Faith in Jesus risen and in our own resurrection; the forgiveness of sins and communion in the Body and Blood of the Lord are not just religious observances. They are the foundation of our lives and the source of energy, joy, enthusiasm for the work of the Lord. A good example of the importance of the witness of the Christian community is the experience of the Jesuit missionaries working among the Huron Indians in Canada. For seven years they lived among the Indians and like them, without a single convert. They finally decided to establish a Christian community, Ste. Marie, which the Indians could observe to their heart's content. It was only then that the missionaries began to have success in their work. The Jesuit *Relations* tell how Ste. Marie became a center for missionary activity for the Jesuits and also a center for the Indians who came for material help and for instruction in the faith. This event in the life of the Church on our own continent illustrates the need of the visible presence of the Church as a communion and a community.

A third point of convergence among the papers was interest in the culture of those receiving the gospel message. The theological basis of this interest is the activity of the Holy Spirit who leads all into truth and who prepares the hearts of those who hear the proclamation. There is also the realization that greater understanding of the mystery of Christ comes as those of various cultures ponder and live it. However, it does seem important not to exaggerate the respect for any human culture to the point where we forget that as a human reality, every culture needs to be judged and corrected in light of the gospel. The temptation to perpetuate Voltaire's myth of the "noble savage" remains alive for us. As Paul said of his own experience, conversion brings a complete reversal of values in the convert's life. For our own people in the United States, the same imperative remains: to be critical of the culture in which we live and to evaluate it in light of Christ. If many are leaving the Church—whether they continue to come to Mass or not—might it be that they have simply adopted the surrounding culture without question? As would-be missionaries, here or there or anywhere, we must likewise be critical of the culture in which we live.

This synthesis began with reference to the missionary effort with which the spread of the gospel began. I would like to conclude by once again looking to those who were missionaries before us, many of whom gave their lives for the sake of those they were evangelizing. I would suggest that we must appropriate our own history and learn from the great missionary efforts of the Church in the past, carried on by Christians who were literally on fire with the love of Jesus Christ. The missionary endeavors of the sixteenth century also merit our study. This includes the work of Ignatius Loyola and his companions in reviving the faith in post-Reformation Europe, as was mentioned by Archbishop Stafford. It also includes the preaching of the gospel in East Asia and in Central and Latin America. Revisionist accounts of these events present the spread of the Christian gospel as a crime in which splendid cultures were obliterated. We need at least to be objective and fair enough to examine the facts to obtain an accurate presentation.

In the last analysis, the gospel is always passed on best by those who let their lives be determined by it, whether they go to foreign missions or not. Francis Xavier was an outstanding missionary whose labors bore enduring fruit in East Asia. Therese of Lisieux, in her Carmel, was afire with the desire to preach the gospel not only in every land, but in every age. We can pray that the Lord will accomplish in us something of what he accomplished in the many Christians who were missionaries before us and that he will raise up many willing to give their very lives in order that all might know the unsearchable riches of Christ Jesus and be transformed in the light of his face. All this for the glory of God and the salvation of the world which he loves.

Authors

Reverend Joseph Augustine DiNoia, O.P., is Associate Professor of Theology at the Dominican House of Studies and Adjunct Professor of Theology at the John Paul II Institute for Studies in Marriage and the Family, both in Washington, D.C. He has also served as Editor-in-Chief of *The Thomist* since 1984. Father DiNoia holds a Ph.D. from Yale University. He has contributed to such books as *Christian Uniquenes Reconsidered, Theology and Dialogue, The Modern Theologians,* and *Speaking the Christian God,* and has published articles in *Theological Studies, Religious Studies,* and *The Catholic Encyclopedia.*

Reverend Avery Dulles, S.J., is currently Laurence J. McGinley Professor of Religion and Society at Fordham University. A leading Catholic scholar, Fr. Dulles has taught at the Catholic University of America (1974–88), Woodstock College (1960–74) and a number of other seminaries and universities across the country. He is the author of fifteen books including *Models of the Church, Models of Revelation, The Catholicity of the Church,* and *The Reshaping of Catholicism,* and has published over five hundred articles on theological topics. Past president of both the Catholic Theological Society of America and the American Theological Society, Father Dulles has been awarded eleven honorary doctorates.

Most Reverend Francis E. George, O.M.I., bishop of Yakima since 1990, served as Vicar General of the Oblates of Mary Immaculate in Rome from 1974 to 1986. He has held a number of positions in the academic world, including Coordinator, Circle of Fellows, at the Cambridge Center for the Study of Faith and Culture and Chairman of the Philosophy Department at Creighton University. Bishop George holds advanced degrees in philosophy, theology, and ecclesiology and has published articles in *SEDOS, Kerygma, The Priest,* and *Vie Oblate.* He is presently a member of the Bishops' Committee on the Missions and on the Board of Directors of the National Catholic Office for Persons with Disabilities.

Sister Joan Frances Gormley, S.S.M.W., is Associate Professor of Scripture at Mount Saint Mary Seminary in Emmitsburg, Maryland. She holds a master's degree in Classics from Harvard University and a doctorate in New Testament Studies from Fordham University. She taught for many years at Trinity College in Washington, D.C., chairing the Theology Department from 1974 to 1983. Sister Gormley has published reviews in *Theological Studies* and the *Fellowship of Catholic Scholars Newsletter*. In 1990 she did research on St. Therese at the Carmelite Convent in Lisieux. Sister Gormley continues to give retreats and to work with a group of young adults associated with Communion and Liberation.

Reverend Eugene LaVerdiere, S.S.S., currently holds the Margaret and Chester Paluch Chair of Theology at the University of St. Mary of the Lake in Mundelein, Illinois, is an adjunct professor of New Testament Studies at the Catholic Theological Union in Chicago, and is senior editor of *Emmanuel Magazine,* where he was editor from 1983 to 1988. He has written several books, including *Luke, The New Testament in the Life of the Church,* and *When We Pray.* Father LaVerdiere is also a consultant for education for the Society for the Propagation of the Faith and a consultant to the Bishops' Committee on the Missions. He holds advanced degrees from John Carroll University, the University of Fribourg, the Pontifical Biblical Institute, and a Ph.D. from the University of Chicago.

Most Reverend William J. McCormack, D.D., was ordained a bishop by Pope John Paul II on January 6, 1987 and is an auxiliary bishop of the Archdiocese of New York. In November 1989, he was elected chairman of the Bishops' Committee on the Missions, National Conference of Catholic Bishops. Since March 1980, he has been the national director of the Society for the Propagation of the Faith. From 1964 to 1970 he was the director of the Society for the Propagation of the Faith for the Archdiocese of New York, and from 1966 to 1971 he served as a member of that society's national board. From 1968 to 1976 he was director of the New York Archdiocesan Office for World Justice and Peace, and from 1970 to 1980 he served as vice chancellor of the Archiocese of New York.

Most Reverend J. Francis Stafford, D.D., has been Archbishop of Denver since 1986. He was named auxiliary bishop of Baltimore in 1976 and bishop of Memphis in 1982. The archbishop has served on many interfaith panels, including the international Oriental Orthodox/Roman Catholic Dialogue, the national Lutheran/Roman Catholic Dialogue, and the Roman Catholic/World Methodist Council Bilateral Dialogue. He has served as chairman of the Bishops' Committee on Ecumenical and Interreligious Affairs and the Commitee on Marriage and Family Life. In 1990, Pope John Paul II appointed Archbishop Stafford a member of the Congregation for the Doctrine of the Faith for a five-year term.

Index

acculturation, 60
Ad gentes (Decree on the Church's Missionary Activity), 9, 21, 33, 36, 56, 58
Angel, Anton, 35
angelism, 63f
Augustine, 19f, 34, 39, 40, 42
autobasileia, 19

Ball, John, 55n.1
Barns, George, 48
basileia, 14, 16
Benedict XIV, 8
Berryman, Philip, 23
Buber, Martin, 77
Buddhism, 82, 91

Carmignac, Jean, 14, 19n.6
Carroll, Janet, 7
catholica, 40
Centesimus annus, 58, 63n.14
Chilton, Bruce, 14
Christian, William A., 82n.19
Clement of Alexandria, 49
collegium, 20
communion, 28f
Congar, Yves, 36, 69n.19
congregatio, 20
Congregation for the Doctrine of the Faith, 37

Council of Constantinople, 49
Council of Laodicea, 49
Cox, Harvey, 22
culture, 9, 11, 55–74, 95
Cyprian, 33, 39

de Lubac, Henri, 40, 41f, 52
Dei verbum (Dogmatic Constitution on Divine Revelation), 72
depositum fidei, 56, 71
Dewey, 64
dialogue, 6, 9, 11, 75–92, 96
Dialogue and Proclamation, 79, 81, 91
Dinoia, J. Augustine, 11, 95f
docetism, 63
Dominum et vivificantem, 43, 68n.17, 69n.18
Donahue, John R., 19
Douglas, Mary, 55
Dulles, Avery, 10, 59, 68n.15, 94f
Dupuis, Jacques, 23, 78n.13, 81, 91

Ecclesiam suam, 70
ekklesia, 16
Emerson, 64
enculturation, 60
Ephrem the Syrian, 94
eschaton, 27

Eusebius, 49
evangelization, 26, 65
  of culture, 58, 61–65

Familiaris consortio, 50, 62
Firth, Raymond, 60n.10
Fitzpatrick, Thomas J., 72
Francis of Assisi, 32
Francis Xavier, 98

Gaudium et spes (Pastoral Constitution on the Church in the Modern World), 17, 21, 29, 43, 44, 46, 56, 57, 58, 69n.18, 71, 72
Geertz, Clifford, 55
Gemeinschaft, 29
George, Francis, 11, 95
German Bishops' Conference, 36
Gesellschaft, 29
Gormley, Joan, 6, 11
Gregory the Great, 20
Gregory XVI, 8
Griffiths, Paul, 88
Grillmeier, Aloys, 34n.3

Harnack, Adolf, 21
Havel, Vaclav, 10
Hilary, 34
Holy Childhood Association, 5
Hugh of St. Victor, 20

Ignatius of Loyola, 46, 72, 98
inclusivism, 81ff, 90ff, 95
inculturation, 6, 11, 58, 60–65, 96
Irenaeus, 33, 41, 49

Jesuit *Relations*, 97
John XXIII, 8, 56, 71
John Paul I, 24
John Paul II, 5, 6, 8f, 10, 11, 24–26, 28, 42, 48, 52, 58f, 62, 68n.16

Katz, Steven, 76n.8
kingdom of God, 6, 9, 10, 13–30, 94f
Knitter, Paul, 23
koinonia, 97
Kung, Hans, 16, 95

LeJay, Claude, 46
Leo XIII, 8
liberation theology, 23
Lumen gentium (Dogmatic Constitution on the Church), 17, 21, 27, 29, 30, 33, 34, 35, 37, 39, 42, 43, 45, 56f
Luther, Martin, 20
Luzbetak, Louis, 56n.1

Mankowski, Paul J., 72
Martins, Jose Saraiva, 60n.11
Masson, J., 60n.11
McBrien, Richard, 22f, 95
McCarthy, Edward, 46
Milbank, John, 75, 81, 83f, 89, 96
missionary spirituality, 6
Mormonism, 64
Mysterium ecclesiae, 34
Mystici corporis, 42

National Conference of Catholic Bishops in the United States, 6, 9
Nicene Creed, 33
Nostra aetate (Declaration on the Church's Relation to Non-Christian Religions), 78, 79, 89
nulla salus extra ecclesiam, 35, 53

O'Connor, James T., 38f
O'Keefe, Donald, 44n.16
On Evangelization in the Modern World, 24
Orientalium ecclesiarum, 34
Origen, 39, 40

Pannenberg, Wolfhart, 15, 16, 23, 95
Papin, Joseph, 17n.4
Paul VI, 24, 25, 58, 62, 70
Perrin, Norman, 14
Piers Plowman, 71
Pius V, 41
Piux XI, 21
Pius XII, 42
Princeps pastorum, 8
Probe nostes (On the Propagation of the Faith), 8
Puebla, 24
Puritans, 21

Quas primum, 21

Ratzinger, Joseph, 35, 37, 40
Rauschenbusch, Walter, 21
Redemptoris missio (On the Permanent Validity of the Church's Missionary Mandate), 5, 8, 10, 11, 24ff, 28, 30, 31, 33, 39, 44, 45, 58, 60, 61n.12, 78f, 83, 88, 89, 90, 94
res, 28
Ricoeur, Paul, 66
Ritschl, Albert, 21
Roman Missal, 41

sacramentum, 28
Salmeron, Alfonso, 46
salvation, 6, 9, 10, 31–54, 95
Samartha, Stanley J., 76
Schnackenburg, Rudolf, 14n.1

Schreiter, Robert J., 55n.1
Schweitzer, Albert, 21
Schwobel, Christoph, 81, 87
secularization, 22
Sharpe, Eric, 77, 84
social gospel, 21
socialization, 60
society, 28f
Society for the Propagation of the Faith, 5
Stafford, J. Francis, 11, 95
Steiner, George, 48n.17
subsistit in, 36ff, 53, 95
Sullivan, Francis, 35, 36f, 95
symbols, 66f

Therese of Lisieux, 98
Thomas Aquinas, 20
To the Ends of the Earth, 5, 9, 10, 11, 69n.20
Turner, Victor, 55
Tylor, Edward Burnett, 55

Ubi arcano, 21
Ubi primum (On the Duties of the Bishop), 8
Unitarianism, 64

Voltaire, 98
von Balthasar, Hans Urs, 52, 68n.17
Vorgrimler, Herbert, 34n.3

White, Leslie, 60n.10
Wojtyla, Karol, 29
World Council of Churches, 17